You And Me No. 1

You And Me No. 1

◆

For Seniors in Love

About Falling in Love Again or Renewing it

Written by Carole and Keith Sheldon

iUniverse, Inc.

New York Lincoln Shanghai

You And Me No. 1
For Seniors in Love

iUniverse, Inc.

For information address:
iUniverse, Inc.
2021 Pine Lake Road, Suite 100
Lincoln, NE 68512
www.iuniverse.com

ISBN: 0-595-29423-5

Printed in the United States of America

Contents

Foreword to the book "You and Me"

By Co-Authors
Carole and Keith Sheldon

Carole and Keith have tried to capture love feelings
For senior lovers like we are which keeps us alive and reeling
We have waltzed through many events in our lives
Like a couple of honey bees buzzing around the hive.
We both lost our life long mates then found each other
We started married life over again as senior lovers, "Oh, brother!."
Our greatest hope is that at any age you, the reader, will love the book
And on our past, present and future books you will get hooked.

No. 1

GOD'S GIFT

Our new-found love is a precious jewel,
A treasure at the center of life's maze
With its twisting paths filled with peril.
My feelings for you cause my world to tremble,
The few hours we spend together not enough.
To have found one another before life's journey is ended
Is truly a wondrous gift from God.
The power of His love for us humbles me.

No. 2

Just Once My Heart

I sit at my computer thinking
Wondering what is really wrong?
I have started to live again,
In my heart I have a beautiful song.
I never thought I would a hear a whisper of love,
But I do and I look around for that Godly dove.
She is standing next to me ready for a crest
Out of me she brings my very best.
I had stopped writing and dreaming about life
Now with her touch all is coming back which is so nice
I thought just once my heart would be alive
But now I know with this beauty I can again jive.
She touched me with a love so deep
And when she touches me, I can't let out a peep.
I thank God and my angel for this new love now
I will foster it into life long adventure somehow.
Just once my heart use to ask
But now in a new love I am about to bask.

No. 3

GOD SAID

I said to God, "Quarter me, cut me in half
I shall arise again as I have in the past.
I will defeat all evil
That has arisen against my love
God is my savior, now and forever more
My love and I shall over evil endure.
History tells us we are free in spirit
As over all we shall dwell
And evil will go to HELL!
We ride on the white stallions into eternity
She on her's and me on mine.
Our love so deep will win over all
Others may think it can be destroyed
But they are wrong!!
We will ride together into Heaven
For God said, "It is so!!"

No. 4

IT ENTERED HER LIFE

A simple computer entered her life
I must say it was really nice.
She told friends to go away
She would talk to them on another day.
She played games of all types
And she played them late into the night.
Soon she could not talk any more
She could not wait to get to a software store.
She learned a new language in her life
Some of it wasn't so nice.
We love her still on this very day.
But day and night on her computer she still does play.

No. 5

NOT THIS TIME

Dear God, I begged of you, not this time.
I have loved two other women, who you took from me.
You called Kari in her prime,
And just recently, you took away Hilda's time.
I love deeply for friends and all
But I hate your death call.
She is one of my dearest friends
And now you threaten her life to end.
I will not have it, so take me instead
For without her I might as well be dead!!
God, you do not need her as a flower in your heavenly garden
Instead at least make her well with a Godly pardon.
She brightens everyone's day with her glorious smile,
Let her dwell with us a long while.
I will gladly give my life for hers
And for whatever purpose it might serve.
I have run my earthly course
But she is like a lighthearted horse.
She is needed here, so My Dear God, make her well,
Band our angels into one I pray tell.
Not this time, Dear God!
We pray for her and keep her on happiness job.
May the skill of doctors be guided by YOUR HAND,
And she will be a joy to all in this land.

No. 6

SWORD DRAWN

God, I have my sword drawn
I will fight any dragon
YOU have sent many to get in my way
But I will slay them all this day.
I walk with my maiden
You cannot have her now
We will love each other more each day.
I have to share her love with others
But never let me with my love her smother
I am very possessive of her
As the kiss she gives alights my heart
And memories of together it starts.
I cannot possess this free spirit I have created
For it was not to be.
I want her to be walking in the way of God
And I shall encourage her to be free.
No one can ever again possess her spirit on this earth
Except for God, she knows at last what she is worth.

No. 7

MY LOVE

There she stood a vision of loveliness
Her smile cast brightest on the mountain background
He was spellbound by her appearance.
He walked away but with a vision
Implanted in his mind.
If he never again held her in his arms
She would forever be his love.
Her lips on his
Had bound his thoughts of her
Forever in his visions of life.
Would they ever walk down life's path together?
Or would they be forced down other roads apart?
He had to caress her every chance he had
Even though it might be sinful in others' eyes.
She was his princess of desire
And he with his white steed
Would pursue her the rest of their lives.
Only God calling each home
Could stop this love.

No. 8

FOUND WHERE YOU ARE

When I searched my heart
I found you there
You were smiling at me
I froze for I was afraid you would disappear
You moved closer till our lips touched
I felt a warming rush to my face
I believe I even blushed
I felt so safe in your arms
No one could hurt us at this time
Yes, I searched my heart
I found you there

No. 9

THROW OF THE DICE

Your soft hand caresses my face
Next your lips and tongue I taste
I feel with you a reckless abandon
How in the world did our love happen?
I wish I could express the deep feelings you create
But I can't for you put me in a motionless state
I know you can over me lord
But my trust for you each day grows more
Why God was so nice to put you in my life
Was it luck or just a throw of his Godly dice?

No. 10

YOUR TOUCH

Your touch each time is heaven sent
As we kiss I am driven to do better in life
Your goodness and kindness make me so proud
As you hold me close when no one else would.
I feel your heart beating in tune with mine
As we gently sway to hidden music known only to lovers
We have to hide our feelings for each other
Most of the time, yet it is there.
Your boundless giving to all makes me
Love you more and more.
I look forward to the touch only you can give
And it is because of that why I still live.
Your independence and free spirit is finally
Showing through and only God knows my love for you.

No. 11

YOUR HEART PLAYING A SONG

Peace upon you
As the year moves along
A smile with pleasant thoughts
And in your heart is playing a song.
Your eyes fixed upon the future ahead
With a love within your heart never to be said
Your feet wanting to dance
And you sway to and fro with your heart playing a song.
You are at peace with your family
They love you so much in their own way
God has touched you and your luck is improve
You laugh out loud for your heart is playing a special song.

No. 12

WANDERING

I wander through each day as aimlessly as one could do
I never know just where I will go.
I try to make contact with my friends
But they really do not understand my plight.
They are loving and caring as I stand before them,
Still I never reveal the pain in my heart.
I am looking for a reason or a new person in my life
Who might just understand where I am heading.
Really I do not know my heading or direction,
Just wishing for another to share this sailing with me.
I cannot take aboard one, who is bound by a bond of hopelessness,
No! I need one who is strong and wish adventure into life as it is.
Where shall I look for such an individual as my heart requests?
There will probably never be an answer to my mess.
I shall continue to look and search for that one person
I need to make her life and mine complete.

No. 13

LOVE CALL TO GOD

I walk about her as a fool
Yet I went a long way in school.
I have met my match in all ways
I would like to spend them with her in the following days.
God, you have taken two flowers from my life
Let me enjoy and love this one, it would be so nice.
She lights up my life with every touch,
God, I don't think that is asking too much.
We walk and talk the same love of life,
If you allow her to love me it would be so nice.
God, you know I can't express all toward her I feel,
But at every chance from her a kiss I steal.
She touches in me the very string of living,
And to her my total love I am giving.
If she should walk away from me tomorrow I would cry,
And ask You, God, why?
God, You put her on earth to give and love,
And at times, in her life, You have taken away that love!
I want only to make her happy the rest of the time,
And whatever she can give me will be just fine.
God, I have learned to love her a whole bunch,
I think you pushed us together, but that is just a hunch.
So God, if you can see it clear,
Keep her close to me, for I love her so dear!!!!

No. 14

WALKING TALL

She walks tall in my heart
I didn't recognize it at the start
She has a smile that lights up my life
And her touch is so nice.
Those soft eyes which change colors with her mood
I would love to kiss her if I could
Poems in my mind come and go
And this love I must take slow
She is a woman like no other
For she has been a wife and mother
When our hands touch a feeling starts to boil
But to make this love work is going to take some toil.
As you read this simple poem
I just thank God for keeping it going.

No. 15

A STROLL

As we strolled down the beach
For your hand I did reach.
Not knowing how to tell you of my love
I whispered a prayer to God above.
Somehow your hand in mine does the trick
For my heart with love begins to tick.
I feel your love for me and mine for you
As we strolled along the ocean's shores.

No. 16

THE KISS

Your mouth on mine
Seduces and compels
Drawing me to you as irresistibly
As the moon draws the tides.
Your kiss kindles overwhelming emotions
Of love and passion yet to be realized.
How I long to tell you of my feelings
But afraid you will think me foolish.
I dream of my lips on yours,
Needing the taste of you to live and
The strength of your arms holding me close;
My longing for you overcoming all else.
Every day I thank God for the miracle of you.

No. 17

SOULMATES

So much in common
Like two halves of the same soul,
Content and at peace with each other.
Our love is like the embers of a fire,
Glowing and warming our hearts.
Your touch ignites the flame at the core of my being;
My dreams filled with endless thoughts of you,
As in my mind I feel your loving arms about me.

No. 18

LOVE ABSOLUTE

How can I deny or ignore the hunger I feel for you?
Your sensuality steals my breath and clouds my mind.
It is difficult not to reach out every time I see you,
Not to touch your loving hands or your gentle face.
My life is no longer my own alone,
So caught up am I in something beyond my control;
A tide washing over me, my love for you
A living thing too powerful to resist.
My daydreams are filled with tantalizing images of tomorrow.
Only God knows what the future holds.
I only know my love for you is absolute.

No. 19

TOUCH ME

Simply, we look forward to touching each other
Attempting to express our true feelings
Is hard at times, still the other person knows.
We will walk in the ways of our ancestors
For our love is right!
Daily and deep problems will be cast aside
For from each other we have nothing to hide.
Touch me, my dear
For I know we have nothing to fear.

No. 20

My All

Will I give her my all,
Yes, I will
Will she give me her all,
Yes, she will
I walk with her on my mind
Yes, all the time.
She does not realize her power
Yes, I know of it all the time.
She touches me with her loving care,
Yes, I feel her everywhere.
We walk together hand and hand
As our hearts begin together to band.
Our lives have changed beyond our belief
We are happy to each other's relief.

No. 21

WALTZING IN LIFE

I can't remember the time I did,
But I did it years ago.
How was I to know a beauty from the East Coast was there
And now for her love I care.
Her hazel eyes at me look,
With them my goose is cooked.
She twists me around her little finger,
And each time my love for her gets bigger.
I am still in command you know!
And which direction she points I go.
Why is it possible to love again?
And hoping it will never end.

No. 22

ANGEL IN YOUR POCKET

I am a tiny angel
I'm smaller than your thumb:
I live in people's pockets
That's where I have my fun.
I don't suppose you've seen me,
I'm too tiny to detect.
Though I'm with you all the time,
I doubt we've ever met.
Before I was an Angel…
I was a fairy in a flower.
God, Himself, hand-picked me,
And gave me Angel power.
Now God has many Angels that
He trains in Angel pools; we become
His eyes, and ears, and hands
We become His special tools.
And because God is so busy,
With way too much to do;
He said that my assignment
Is to keep close watch on you.
When He tucked me in your pocket
He blessed you with Angel care;
Then told me to never leave you,
And I vowed always to be there.

by
Anonymous

No. 23

FEELING JOY

For three lonely years I had lived within myself
Waiting for my allotted days to pass.
Now you have given new meaning and joy to my life.
Love is the most wonderful feeling the world has to offer;
You have captured my heart with your loving touch,
And your intoxicating kisses have my doubts won over.
You heat my senses and send my thoughts spinning away.
I fear at times by my direct words I embarrass;
For that I am sorry, but subtle games I do not know how to play.
There's no one in the world I want more than you.
In my quiet way there is only one thing left to say—
I love you

No. 24

PRIDE

Yes, I am proud,
Proud to know that you love me,
Wanting to build with you new memories.
Your beautiful words of love I hold close to my heart,
Cupid has pierced my soul with love's dart.
My feelings for you are so deep and true,
My hands and lips cannot resist showing my love for you.
Please know you can trust me, for I will never hurt you,
A beautiful love was born when our kindred spirits touched.
Your loving ways have set my passions free,
My love, you are everything to me.

No. 25

SHOULD YOU WANT TO GO

If you find I am not the one,
And you feel you have to run.
Don't be afraid,
I understand for I gave.
You must live the life you choose,
I will try not try to have the blues.
You were an important part of my life,
And for the short time it was really nice.
We are grown adults, I am sure,
I want for you what you want forever more.
Life gave us a few wonderful moments along the way,
But for them you don't have to pay.
Be gone on your journey in life,
Knowing you was really nice.
I regret not one moment with you,
Now, may you in your selecting of life be true

No. 26

FLOWER OF LIFE

All well and good, you say to yourself
But you will never put the good times on a shelf.
No, you place them into the special place
Which over time you will share them with another.
We need to move ahead and if God decides
You need another mate then it shall be.
You can love and hold in your heart some of the past
But the future is what God wants you have and enjoy.
Share your remaining love with another
Even if it is for just a few moments or years.

No. 27

A SPECIAL MAN

My man is a most amazing man.
A talented poet and writer unparalleled,
He has a sparkling wit and sweet smile;
With a generosity of spirit he brightens our world.
He shares with all his life, his laughter and his love;
His compassion encompasses all those less fortunate.
A man who cares deeply for his family, he is
A loving parent and devoted grandparent without equal.
He is a kind and caring human being
With a strong belief in his church and God.
Having him near completes my life;
He is my Special Friend.

No. 28

WHEN YOU LOVE

Do you wonder what goes on when you're falling in love?
Does time really stop?
Does it really matter?
When your lips touch another
Do you think or care what was taught you by your mother?
When rain is falling all about
Is it then you two try to make out?
Do you worry what others think
Probably not because their thoughts will stink!
Love must be just right
And you know it when holding each other tight.
So when you love, be true to each other
And all will be perfect in time.

No. 29

YOU WALK IN THE WAYS OF A QUEEN

You touch so many others
As you walk along the way.
You are fair and careful in judgment of another
Still you are so helpful in the time of need.
Many queens in the past did not have your qualities
Yet they led others along life's path.
You push ahead without fear
Your help to where you are is so dear.
For various reasons people can not say what they feel
But from you strength and love they steal.
Please continue being yourself while picking up so many friends
As you pass along in this tangled web of life.
There are not many like you so you are very rare
As a precious jewel that passes by in our lives.
We are so proud to have you pass by
And know God sent you and ask Him silently why?

No. 30

A Silent Life

As one who has lost a loved one
You pass into a silent life.
You search the past for your loves
And know they are no more.
Still they dance in your head and you wonder
What were they really like?
Were they happy or just sad in their presentation
Did they make happiness for the one who has gone?
You search the dream for a smile or a laugh or two
Still the question is not answered when it is through.
Silent life wraps around you while in the dead of night
And you might shake with an uncontrollable fright.
At night the other side of the bed is so cold
But over there you roll as if you are still in control.
Everyone who has lost a loved one like you
Tells you in time you will see it through.

No. 31

LOTS OF WATER

A beautiful flower needs lots of water,
As does a flower of life.
If this flower does not receive the needed water
It dries up and dies as does the flower of life.
We behold the beauty of a blooming flower
And do not understand why it does so.
It attracts bees and other insects with its beauty
Yet it has much more than that.
A flower of life has the same attraction and needs
And without them its death it does speed.
Lots of water can mean many things
But our flower of life to our heart sings.
We shall do our best to water our flower of life
With what it requires to continue its beauty.
We are just hanging on as long as we can
To our own flower of life may it be a spouse or child.

No. 32

HANGING ON

When one hangs on to a hopeless love,
It is sad, but a fact of life.
Sometimes, God encourages a mismatch in life
Just to get one to the true love of their future.
Why this happens is one of the mysteries of life
It seems all is perfect then that stranger walks in.
God has somehow used one to position another into a renewed life
Why this attraction comes about is God's way.
The loser is not the one who has lost for that was his purpose,
Instead it is the love pain caused by this mystic reunion.
The loser knew from the beginning he was destined to give,
And is in a way real happy his part made his ex-love happy.
This is life's fact and not always apparent to those involved,
But it does happen to bring about a few moment of true love.

No. 33

SMILING HAZEL EYES

She casts a spell upon all who meet her
As those smiling hazel eyes spellbind a person.
She is unaware of the power her eyes cast
Only that she loves others and wants love in return.
She has enjoyed parts of her life
While other times has struggled to survive.
As she continues along life's path
She gathers in new friends with her bubbling smile.
She remains loyal to all and loves her children very deeply
And forgives those who have hurt her along the way.
She makes one forget toils of life thus wanting only to be around her
As she makes life worth living with her giving.
This is a type of person who we need more of
And less of the hateful ones.
We are so blessed to have this Lady among us
For she cares, loves and works to make one feel good.
Those smiling hazel eyes and smile upon her face
Makes us happy to be part of the human race.

No. 34

THANK YOU

Thank you for today and every day.
You have enriched my life beyond measure.
Supporting me with loving encouragement,
You inspire me to reach for heights as never before.
Having you near fills me with joy and pride.
You light up my day with your wit and smile;
Sweet kisses and touches holding me at your side.
With your charm and tales of times past you beguile.
You are in my head and my heart and under my skin
So deeply you feel like a part of me.
Is it any wonder I love you so?

No. 35

WALTZ ME AROUND AGAIN

His head was spinning,
Her heart was saying this is a new beginning.
Her glowing hazel eyes and that radiant smile,
Made his heart skip a beat once in a while.
As they waltzed around the dance floor,
Into her eyes he looked deeply as never before.
He shocked as to his ability to keep pace,
For his knees felt weak as he looked into her lovely face.
"Waltz me around again, my dear,
For I love holding you so near."
She spoke ever so softly,
"Darling, this dancing is so costly,"
"My sweet dear, waltzing is still done here,"
He answered as the two danced on holding each other so near.
Far in the distance of the past,
Had been forgotten at last.
He waltzed her around again on the dance floor,
For apart they would never be anymore.

No. 36

MAGIC

Whisper to me softly of love
As your gentle hands touch me,
Holding me close to your heart.
The beauty of your words shakes my world,
Showing me the paradise that awaits us.
Your kisses bewitch me until I cannot think.
I am in a state of enchantment,
My mind conjuring visions of heaven.
You have captivated me body and soul;
Your touch mesmerizes me,
Taking me to that magical place
Where dreams of complete love come true.

No. 37

OUR STORY

You must have been a beautiful baby
You must have been a wonderful child
Oh! Baby just look at you now!!
When I am near you this song
Tingles and dances through my mind.
Strange how most of our lives
We never knew about the other.
How we recently worked at the same place
Yet unwisely I never looked deeply into your face.
When the blindness was removed from my eyes
There you were in all your glory
And now together in life will it be a different story?

No. 38

SENSATIONS

Tenderly or with the sweet intensity of passion
Your touch heats my skin,
Creating a deep physical stirring
And a bittersweet yearning to be closer to you.
The sensuous magic of your hands
Causes my body to throb with exquisite sensation,
Making me feel like something more than a woman.
Do you feel the same emotions when we embrace?
Do my hands give you the same pleasure?
We each tread so gingerly down future's path,
Will we dare the fates with our new love I wonder.
I must believe we have the strength to face the future together,
With a deepening love in our hearts to show the way.

No. 39

FEEL THE FLOW

I walked straight into the heart of another
I must be careful for I have no right to hurt them.
Remember it is their heart and not yours
Tread lightly as you go.
If truly you feel the flow
The love will bounce between you two, back and fro.
Hold this love with care and pride
For a broken heart makes you think you have died.
Yes, tread lightly as you two go
If true you will feel the loving flow.
A right match at any age is super
Feed it and don't be a party pooper!!!

No. 40

COMING HOME

Your look of love is like a tender kiss on my soul;
I am staggered by the beauty of it.
So much of my mind is filled with you,
The dreams, the questions, the possibilities.
There are times I am frightened
By something so powerful it has taken over my life.
Seemingly urgent and unstoppable,
I feel consumed by our love.
All I ask for my remaining days
Is to have your arms embrace me.
I don't know how this love happened.
I only know that in your arms I am home.

No. 41

SAY IT WITH WORDS

You write but say what you mean
I want to be mean and lean.
I want her to drool over me
But those days have passed from my living scene
I look at her as a young fraile beautiful thing
Does she see the same scene?
I doubt mentally we can go back
And that one thing I know as a fact.
Still our dreams can drift on
And her beauty now is what I am very fond.
The things she does to me would have never been
In her youth way back when.
It must have been in God's plan for she and I
And may it last until we both are taken into the sky.

No. 42

A SUNDAY DRIVE

I think of our drive yesterday,
The way we laughed at our silliness
And the sheer joy of enjoyment.
The time I spend with you has a quality
None other has for me—life is good.
A blending of spirits sends
A thrill of excitement through me.
A caring and sensitive man,
I know I can trust you with my love.
Remembering the texture of your skin
Beneath my hand,
Sensual feelings wind through me-
A wonder of sensations in full flood.
I am caressed by your soft brown eyes,
Your kisses a tender assault on my senses.
Thank you for your love.

No. 43

OUR LOVE

Dear God, I was wondering
About my love how I am blundering?
Do I try too hard in my foolish way?
Do I fail because the right words I don't say?
Of course, my love and I aren't failing
It is just on unchartered waters we are sailing.
Each of us has trouble expressing true feelings
For in each other's arms sends our emotions reeling.
Yes, God for us find a way,
For our love for each other grows deeper each day.

No. 44

A NEW WORLD

You have a strength and gentleness that creates sweet lightning;
The need for you thunder shaking my entire being.
I get lightheaded being close to you,
Breathing your scent, tasting you;
The depth of my hunger for you all consuming.
My thoughts of you make me blush,
My self-control shattered by your touch,
Creating an explosion of heat deep within me.
When I embrace you I hold the world in my arms.
Will you and I share the excitement of a new world?
I pray we will find the way,
But if shadows fill our life, may we be wise
And let love illuminate our path.

No. 45

FLOATING ON A CLOUD

My head is spinning,
And a great event I am winning.
I am floating on a cloud in the sky so high,
I am so lucky and wonder why?
Was it my hard practice and long hours of training?
Soon on my head compliments will be raining.
It is once in a life time I am enjoying,
Or with fate am I toying.
I think not!
I worked hard, trained well and had a plan,
I followed my heart and did the best I can.
Victory and celebrations may be short lived,
Yet I shall now enjoy all my accomplishment did.
I must remember not to for long on this dwell,
For ahead the challenge to win is tough as HELL!

No. 46

LOVE AND LAUGHTER

Do I love too deeply, too fiercely?
It frightens me, my need for you
My desire for you overpowering.
Every day with you memorable;
Each moment together a gift that must not be wasted.
Our fingers entwined, your touch steals my breath away.
Your loving nature expressed in so many ways,
The sensual feelings you arouse with your caressing hands,
Your sweet kisses addictive, your brown eyes seductive.
You've given me strength and taught me to trust again.
Over time the love I have for you has deepened
Until it's like something alive inside me.
You make me laugh with joy and happiness.
Love and laughter you have given me,
The two most precious gifts in the world.
For me you are the very essence of love.

No. 47

SOMEHOW

I saw a beauty walking among the people
I had not noticed her before.
I was blinded by my big nose
It seems to get in my way at times.
Suddenly I found a true friend
She had been there all along.
I am sorry I was so ignorant in my thoughts
But what is important I have found her now.
Her hazel eyes pierce my heart strings
And I want to hold her each day
But I know that is impossible in a sense
But not true in the future tense.
We shall walk together as many do
For finally I have found a love that is true!!

No. 48

YOU ARE

You are my drive
You are my heart
You are my soul
Your touch drives me forward
You are my reason for wanting to succeed
You have the lips I love to press
You make each day worth living
You are the crazy one who listens when I know you are bored
You have the eyes that make me truthful
You have the soul that should make God proud
You are the one now who I adore
You are the one who makes me proud of myself
You are the one who God said, "straighten out his soul!!"
You are the ONE!!!

No. 49

MOVE ON

Life has its ups and downs
At times it is serious and others it is for clowns.
I for one love the clowning time
For that is when to others you are kind.
Moving on in life is so important to us all
And being that part clown I have a ball.
My love and I are quite alike you know
For both of us like to be on the go.
Where we journey on our little trips
Makes for us together our hearts skip.
When love is so grand and having a clown's fun
Makes for time with you so grand, my hon!

No. 50

DESTINY

Some things are meant to happen,
In their own time and in their own way.
Our love is new; let life be kind, I pray.
God, watch over us and lead us
To a place where we'll be safe;
On the right path guide us with your Grace.
In stormy times let my arms give him comfort.
Let me give him of my strength if life's seams come apart,
For this man holds in his hands my heart.

No. 51

WALKED INTO MY LIFE

When you walked into my life
I was not aware.
I was so dumb I did not even
Believe or care.
One day I awoke and you were there
We found for each other we cared.
After our long drive of this day
You listened to my bragging way.
Once I got home I thanked GOD for you
Each day I am feeling our love is true.

No. 52

A SYMPHONY

Our love is music no one else can hear;
A beautiful flower opening to the sun,
Meant for our eyes only.
You awake in me feelings I've not felt in so long,
A storm of emotions stirred by your touch.
Your kisses excite my senses,
Making me want you more with each day that passes.
I thank God for hearing my prayer,
Our symphony of love a gift to cherish.

No. 53

WANTING YOU

I think of you with shivers of anticipation through me rippling
And the warmth that fills me when I look at you
A tender whirlwind in my heart spinning.
What spell have you cast over me?
I feel like a naive child again,
Overwhelmed by the need for you.
The scent of you on my skin
An aphrodisiac unlike any other,
Igniting the need to be drawn even closer to you,
Wanting you until I can't breathe.
I dream of the day when I will be yours true,
Awakened from sleep by your sweet kisses and loving touch,
Greeting the new day from the protective warmth of your arms
And peace filling me all the way to my soul.

No. 54

MY LADY SO PROUD

I love you my Lady So Proud
I cry my love to you out loud.
You laugh at my stupid words and jokes
And say I should share them with other folks.
When I am with you my mind dances with lovely thoughts
And in a blinding love I find myself wrapped and like a fish caught.
Your touch upon my head drives me nuts and somewhat wild
And yet in your embrace I am like a helpless child.
Where did you come from all of a sudden in my life?
Still I love you and feel next to you so nice.
Why do I even question your very being?
For in your eyes a deep love for me I am seeing.
Your ability to correct my words of text and make them seem so great
Yet my holding on to them makes them nothing, is that our fate?
My Lady So Proud I love you with all my heart
And again I ask, "Where did it all start?"

No. 55

TO MY SPECIAL FRIEND

I have looked into a mirror
And can not see anything that you would want to love.
Still, I have a weird sense of humor
About nearly anything, and you are willing to enjoy it.
Does that mean others are not listening to the humor
Or is it possible you are wise beyond all others.
I sit here listening to my many country western stars
And your love for the classics will we enjoy the same in time
I feel a love which can win over all
And both of us for that love will not let it fall!!
I see a beautiful lady with the most precious hazel eyes,
Our life long partners have gone to a place in Heaven
But does mean that our love for each other should not have a place to vent?
I think God has crashed us together for a purpose
What it is neither of us are sure but He will tell us in time.
I pull my belt a little tighter to impress you
I never had what it will take, maybe I will walk a little straighter.
You are as pretty as any young lady in my past has been
But now you are wiser and I have to be careful of my moves in the end.
I know we walk together down the last path in our life
But being with you really makes it nice.
I love you, my Special Friend
And we are together until the end....

No. 56

STUBBORN MAN

Have you ever met a man as stubborn as me?
Every time you attempt to pay me back I flee!
I love you more deeply than you know
But a pay back makes me run and go!
You are stuck with a nut of sorts
For when you ask "How much" I race off in my shorts.
"What am I to do with you?" you ask.
I respond, "Be my special friend of whom I am very fond."
I tried not to rhyme this in my love call to you
But it didn't work so forgive I still love you so true!!.

No. 57

WILL YOU?

Will you come to me in the early morning hours?
Will you wake me with sweet kisses and tender caresses?
Will you share with me the depth of your love?
Will you hold me until the sun rises above?
Going up my spine is a shiver of temptation
As through me sizzles warm, delicious anticipation.
Tell me, am I too bold?
My love is yours to cherish and to hold.
I am by all the possibilities dazzled,
Wound about by silken threads of desire
For a man whose loving nourishes my soul.
I, too, am shy and uncertain,
But I know our love will overcome all.

No. 58

A SENIOR LOVE

Why is it they hold hands while they walk?
Why do they look into each other's eyes with total love?
I can not imagine their plight
For now I find myself in that twilight.
She has lost her partner of many years
And so have I.
We look for love in another dimension
And our wild thoughts of each other we never mention.
We loved our partners of many years,
And over their loss we shed many tears.
We were left here to struggle on
And of each other we have become very fond.
I feel a complete love overcoming my very frame
And of it with her I have no shame.
GOD, must have made it and approved of it for sure
Now of her I want much more.
GOD walk us through the difficult times
For in your light our love does shine.
Her very touch sets me aflame
And when I feel love for her I am not ashamed.
I know this is a crazy poem to express my love
But I don't care for I know it has been blessed from above.

No. 59

HOW

Would we meet under different conditions?
Would we love each other so much?
Could you follow me around to all the ball games?
Would you adopt my grandkids as I have?
Or would you say where are you taking me?
I think you would love me no matter what
You would go to my ball games for you see your past
We both know life forever will not last!
We huddle when no one is looking
But in our hearts there is a love cooking!!
I thank you, for your love and being with me
As no one else has ever done in many years.
I will provide you with a cover as no one else can
For you have been a special person who will stay with me to the end.

No. 60

AIR OF MYSTERY

You enjoy an air of mystery about me
But it is not real you know.
I am just a simple soul of sorts
When I love I fully do you court.
Yes, I love your touch so soft and nice
And I pass it off saying, "It is my body lice!"
I have never been so confused about what to do next
You are so precious in my later years.
I am no longer wild with my hands and caressing
Instead I fumble around looking for what to do next.
I guess it comes from a long time out of the love game
And I never was so good I had gained any fame.
Love me and show me the way
For I love you more each day

No. 61

I WALK

You are my love
You are there to help me keep alive
You smile at me when I am wrong
Yet I know I love you
You correct me when I am wrong
Still for your love I long
I walk silently along the path
For I know now it will last.
You smile when I am wrong
And in your heart I feel a different song.
I lacked it a long time
A type of love you give freely to me
I want you to love me yet I must love you the same way
I feel each time I hold you it is there
And I enjoy your pressing against me
That you feel the same for me
In strange unable to describe feeling.
I am unable to totally love you all the way,
It may happen some day!!!!
I want to but I feel now I am still held back
My restraint may be personal in a way you may not understand.
The month of March will come to a close.
Then my fear of life might end.

No. 62

THE GLORY OF YOU

You have awakened in me a need and desire
That I didn't know I possessed.
You have gotten into my blood
And I am incapable of rational thought.
A warmth and tenderness burns through me
At the glory of your touch;
I am oblivious to all but you.
My dreams are filled with the wonder of being together;
The fascination of you.
A short time ago I didn't know you,
Now your very existence
Is the most important thing in my life.
My days begin with thoughts of you
And end with desire for you.
So much in love with you that life
Without you would be meaningless.
I glory in your love!

No. 63

KNOW NOT

I know not what God wants me to write
To blame him for some of my stuff is not right.
To believe what he does is all okay
I do believe that may be the right way.
To have a special friend like you
Is what I write to you for is mainly true.
We walk among the friends and unknown with a love and pride
If we love each other, then I have gone to Heaven and died.
Why this happened so late in life
Is still very nice.
Your touch makes me enjoy life again
I can't wait to see you and wonder when?
May you have a wonderful time in this life
And to share it with you is really nice.

No. 64

BLUSH NOT MY BEAUTY

I see your beautiful hazel eyes
As they softly search my face for love
Which often does not appear.
I hide my feeling deep within my soul
For what reason I do not know.
It could be a fear of life
Or just my stupid way of expressing my love.
I feel a deep relationship with you
Still I hold my deepest love in reserve
As a military general does his best troops.
There are many thoughts racing through my mind
As we kiss and hold each other
I wonder if I give all will I soon lose another?
We have so much in common
And I know this to be so true
I would never do anything to hurt you!!
Time is not really on our side
So I am trying very hard my emotions not to hide.
You are so patient with me that I love
So if I do some weird thing
Still I love you and in Heaven it will ring!!
Blush not my beauty at my weird remarks and moves
For they are all done not to upset but to show my love for you.

No. 65

MY LOVELY SPECIAL FRIEND

I am sending you a wildwood kiss
I feel your love in my heart
For that is where true love starts.
I watch your eyes out stare me time after time
I feel like a lost soul still searching.
I look out my dirty windows at the pure wind blowing
Through the trees causing emotions in my soul.
I feel your touch caressing my neck
And my heart jumping up and down with each stroke.
How can I ever repay you for my love for you
Will it be with a special touch or caressing I can deliver?
I wait your touch and whisper that will tell me
What would please your very soul.
I am shy
And with you I wonder why?

No. 66

THE BEACH

We find the beach on the ocean
So inviting for beauty and love.
The birds glide overhead
As we find our love alive and not dead.
The sand pushes up between our toes
As walking along the water's edge we go.
Being Seniors in life we still walk hand in hand
Thinking as we go what a wonder time and land.
Your hand in mine
What a wonderful time.
We know not what others think
But our hearts are in tune as in our love we drink.
You laugh at my stupid thoughts and words
And we know our love words by others are heard.
We care not as we walk
For again in our late life it is just small talk.

No. 67

YOUR HAND

Your hand on my cheek
A quick kiss I would sneak.
Your touch calms my very being
In your eyes a beautiful love I am seeing.
As you sit and enjoy the tossing of the surf
I think of your first.
In your heart you travel to your past
Knowing once you leave it the dreams won't last.
You are wrong you know
For once again waves will return to you a private show.
Let not go of your wonderful past I say
For our future ahead by God is already cast.

No. 68

STUMBLE

She strokes gently on my day old stubble
And I know my heart is in trouble.
Her hand playfully rubs the back of my neck
Thoughts of love rumble within me saying what the heck!!
She toys with my short hair on my head
My excitement arouses and I know I am not dead.
How can this woman do this to me?
Keep it up to her I silently plea.
When we embrace she holds me so tight
I am helpless unable to fend her off or fight.
From her love I stumble across the computer keys
Unable to write another verse if you please.

No. 69

I SWOON

It looks so inviting as I peer across an open field of green
It is one of the most expressive and beautiful to be seen.
To write about this common view in U.S.A.
Can be short or written about all day.
Our love is much the same
It is an emotion hard to explain.
I look into her eyes for an answer to my plight
And wish to hold her ever so tight.
When my emotions take leave and into flight
I know I am wanting to hold her all night!
Some trees stand straight and tall
But for me I want her love most of all.
I can see her gliding across a ballroom floor
With the grace of a ballerina and much more.
Her touch is so smooth on my neck
So to the rest of the world I say, "What the heck!"
How can this creature do this to me?
Is my spirit is captured and no longer free?
She would never wish that for me
No! She makes me a better person, you see!!
I will write more about this wonderful lady soon
But for now I just am amazed at her and swoon!!!!

No. 70

KEITH

You say I don't need you
I need only you with every fiber of my being!
How do I make you understand?
You electrify me, thrill me with your love.
A man beyond compare, you light up my life
And give meaning to my existence.
An exquisite melody to our song of love,
Your poetry arouses my deepest feelings.
My senses excited by your touch
She sensations stirred by your kisses enthrall.
I need your love to sustain me;
I will always love and need you.
My heart is in your keeping.

No. 71

WHEN THE WORLD CRASHED

You walked in when my world seemed to crash
You smiled and said, "Can I help or go with you?"
No one else seemed to care even though they cared
So I helplessly took your hand for your strength.
As time moved on I realized your love
I thought at times I could never return it
Still you cared not but just kept being there
You turned around my hate to a deep love
For I had failed and now it mattered not to you
As you without a word guided me back to life
I wonder why I was so lucky to have God placed you before me.
Maybe you were searching as I
And we just finally found each other.
No matter it makes a great deal of difference
In our limited time on this earth.
God is Great! He does strange things many times
How he had time for you and I is a great thing
The fact is he did and now we must make the most of it
As we walk together down the final path of life.

No. 72

LOVING

I have placed my love and trust in the palms of your hands,
My soul opening to you as a flower to the sun.
Glorious sensations assault my senses,
Your mouth on mine giving overwhelming pleasure,
The taste of you as intoxicating as wine.
Your hands on me strong, sure and exciting,
Making every nerve sing with desire.
I want only to hold you, touch you, kiss you,
Consumed by an aching need for your loving.
The vibrations between us strong and powerful,
You touch a place within me
That no one has touched for a long time.
You make my heart smile.

No. 73

POTATO

This is dumb as I write

For I am preparing my supper potatoes tonight.

You are like a potato you know

For you are my favorite everywhere I go.

What fool can compare you to a favorite

Still your kisses and touch I really savior it.

I am about as romantic as a toad

But remember in many fairy tales the toad won the princess's toes.

I am not sure I sure I should have rhymed it that way

But I love you each and every day.

When we touch I know I am not in command

And to myself I say, "Oh! Damn!"

Your amazement at what I may say next

Puts on me a sort of hex.

I try hard not to say anything dumb

But when I am with you I feel like sucking my thumb.

I am a babe in your arms

And with you I feel out of any harm

Yes, I am a potato of sorts

And I love you for your laughter and being a good sport.

No. 74

MISCHIEF

You say I get a twinkle in my eye
But dear it is only a reflection of you.
I never stir up comedy just for you
It jumps out because I love your laughter so much.
You encourage me to believe in myself
But no matter how I try to stop making you laugh I can't!!
Your expressive eyes light a torch in my heart
And I want you near for in my life you are an important part.
Most of all when I do something rather stupid
You think it isn't and laugh at my boyish attempts for you.
Why our match came about I don't question
I am just glad it did!!

No. 75

MY SWEETIE PIE

My Sweetie Pie, life with you has been
Like having life on a silver platter
You are nice as pie
And sharp as a tack
You have always been
Neat as a pin
You are as proud as a peacock
And always on time, right on the dot
You know you have been
The apple of my eye
You are one in a million
Also I think you are cute as a button
Your kisses are as sweet as honey
Your body is a right smart piece of art work
Your touch is as soft a silk
And your skin is as clear as any crystal
Yes, your as cute as a bug's ear
You are as merry as a lark
Your ideas are as fresh as a daisy
And you are mostly busy as a bee
You are as innocent to life as a new born babe
Yet you purr like a kitten next to me
You generally have me between the devil
And the deep blue sea
To me, you are a real prize winner
For with you I never know which end is up
Lots of times I would give a penny for your thoughts
While under stress you are so cool and collected

Your laughter is like a singing lark
I get a real kick out of it
You tickle the socks off me
And I love it when you feel your ginger
Yes, You are my Sweetie Pie!!

No. 76

LONGING

When you call me sweetheart I feel so loved
And your poetry sends exquisite thrills through me.
I have an inability to say aloud what is burning inside,
To put into words the compelling fascination you hold for me.
I need to touch you, hold you, kiss you.
I miss you when we are not together,
The ache of longing unbearable.
I see your face in my mind, hear your voice,
Remembering how you taste and feel.
With you I am lost to love and passion, dreams and desire.
I cannot conceive of us not being together.
Could you possibly love me as much as I love you?
You've slipped into my heart as softly as a whisper,
You fill my heart with happiness.

No. 77

OUR MOVIE SPEAKS

Today when we saw the movie "Princess' Diary"
I felt just maybe it was the two of us
Not knowing how to be true lovers in a way.
There is no formal training I know of as with the princess
Still we are afraid we might be wrong in our attempts.
It is not the kissing or holding each other
Our love is much deeper than that.
Our caring about each other and wanting to make sure the other is okay
Willing to push when needed and when to back off.
You are such an important person in my life
And I love your touch even though you think at times I don't.
As I pound away at my keyboard I feel your guidance in what I write
And it makes for me a very happy and loving night.
Good night my sweet and pleasant dreams be yours
For I am yours and being with you is top priority in my life.

No. 78

SAME WAVE LENGTH

It amazes both of us when one speaks
And the other was thinking exactly what was said.
The twinkle in each other's eyes when this happens
Makes us laugh plus scares each of us about this event.
Is it we are on the same lover's wave length?
Maybe it is just an unexplained event in our lives
But both of us have lived long enough that it gives us the hives.
We really don't want it to be explained at this stage of the game
Still our thoughts of each other we don't want someone else to claim.
So we will for the time being say we have come to the same wave length
And in that way we feel our love gains strength.

No. 79

BOUNCE AROUND

We get so tickled over when we get out of the car
After a long drive and try to get our sense of balance.
We stagger for a moment under the influence of our medication
Which has caused us to be unbalance for a short time.
We suppose our love is not causing it but it just might
Once we have a step or two we find all it okay and right.
Each of us attempts to bounce around the vehicle to each other
But we break into a laugh until our sense of balance has recovered.
Our God who is high in the sky will have quite a pair
When the two of us finally get the call to be there.
We suppose all Senior lovers have this same event in their later lives
For each have medication and their balance at times takes all they have to give.
We offer our advice to the younger if they will listen
For still in Senior lives the deepest love can still glisten.

No. 80

WAVING LOVE

Why do I walk away when I don't want to?
Is it a waving love coming from our past?
Do we feel a tug from those of the past we have loved?
Or is it just because we have forgotten how to love?
One never really knows the answers each day
we just love as best we can—each in our own way.

No. 81

ALWAYS

I was in darkness until you came to me
Alone no more, lonely no longer
When I hold you I have everything I need.
You cloud my senses until there is nothing but you.
I love you for your caring heart, your humor and sharp wit,
Your gentle hands and your willingness to share my burdens.
Because of you I am living with love and joy.
Your love leaves my heart shaking;
You're the reason I breathe, the one I live for.
Your eyes make to me seductive promises
And in my dreams you unlock a world of delight and wonder.
Life goes by so fast, let us hold on to what is important.
You are my forever, be with me always.

No. 82

KING OF HEARTS

You are my King of Hearts
You've made my life a fantasy come true.
Your kisses remind me of how much I need you,
The heat of you, your body against me pressed,
Your hands loving me so sweetly.
The intense power of you stops my breath.
I feel your love inside me shining,
Making me feel I can do anything.
I still find it hard to believe you truly love me
Until I read the poetry you've written so beautifully.
To our love and our future together I am committed.
My heart overflows with love for you.

No. 83

SENIOR LOVE AFTER DEATH

I wandered around in a fog
I walked to a local pond and talked to a frog
My wife and partner had died suddenly leaving me
She didn't have a time to say good-bye I hated it you see!
The frog said nothing that made sense
So from there I walked away and clung to a fence
I didn't know where to turn since my wife had quickly died
Then I saw another in the same situation and to her I cried.
I was totally wrong for she sang a different love song
She loved another but decided to string me along
I was such a fool in my desperate love making
But this woman was not giving and only taking
It was then along came a wonderful lady of the time
And she was patient in straightening me out just fine.
How can a fool ever say thank you to a great woman?
I guess the only way is "Thank You" dear friend forgive me for being so stupid!!
We have so much in common in life
And that makes life so wonderful and nice.
I think as we walk together in our final journey
It will be worth all that life has to offer in our life's turning.

No. 84

FEELINGS

Do you truly realize the depth of my feelings for you?
Your kisses create a longing in me to be a part of you,
The feelings I have for you amazing, thrilling and sweet.
I want to reach out to you, giving you all my love,
Having you hold me close to you,
To feel your heat and inhale your scent.
The emotions you excite deep in my heart overpowering,
I can't stop touching you, the temptation sharp and insistent.
The intensity of the feelings you arouse with a look or a touch
Like a spark to dry grass, igniting a fire within me,
The chemistry between us explosive.
It is your love, your sweet caring, that gives my world meaning.
I need you in my life for whatever time remains to us.
My heart is lost to you.

No. 85

A NEW SONG

Life can surprise you in many ways
And, where you don't imagine, you can meet happiness.
Loneliness never smiles and was not a choice I made.
Now, because you are here my life is changing.
It's you in my dreams and plans—and in my fantasies.
The power of your love bursts through me like glorious sunshine.
I thank God for what you are, for what you give me,
For a simple kind of love that is deeper than ever before.
I exist for you, your touch, your smile, your kiss;
The joy of being with you, of having you beside me.
When you caress me I feel a wild glory.
You're the words and the music of a new song,
My hymn of love.

No. 86

FOREVER

Does you heart race when I am near?

Do you throb with desire when we touch?

Do you dream about what real intimacy between us could be like?

All these things you do to me.

You have captured my mind and my heart.

I can think of little else.

We seem to fit so well, it seems so natural.

Like stardust your love showers me with a magical joy.

You brought sunshine into my life

And chased the shadows away.

Thank you for loving me.

I surrender to you.

No. 87

ONLY YOU

When I'm feeling lonely I look inside my heart-
I find your love nestled there and I feel great joy.
I have been alone and untouched for too long.
The feel of your hand on my skin awakens
A longing that is deep and powerful.
Your touch starts a primitive need sweeping through me;
I want to stroke you with the gentle caress of a lover,
Sensual feelings sliding through my body.
You stir my blood and images spin in my mind,
There is a hunger in me, a desire for you.
Breathless at the thought of the power you have over me,
I can't think for wanting you—only you.
I need you to love me.

No. 88

TWO SPIRITS

You walked right into my heart.
Every time I look at you I fall in love with you again.
You are everything I want—you are the music in my life.
I love you so much I feel it in every pore of my body.
I want to be touched by you, to know that you want me.
Your touch, your kiss creates a stunning whirlwind of sensation,
Excitement explodes through me, making me feel reckless.
The taste of you potent, drawing me closer,
The ache of wanting you intense.
Beyond passion, love is a merging of spirits,
A generosity of the soul.
Love is the source of life.

No. 89

YOU GAVE ME BACK MY LIFE

Where does one go to find life after the death of a lifelong partner?
First you look within yourself and where you are at
Then you look around at relatives and friends
You search for someone who can again turn your life into happiness
Many times there seems to be no one that can do it
For you are bound by a sense of loyalty to your past partner and lover
You fumble and many times taken in by a gold digger of sorts
But our God finds a way to straighten you out
For out there somewhere is another looking just like you
We make the greatest mistake as we look far when love is near.
I found myself doing that until I looked beyond my nose
And there from nowhere my senior love arose.
She was an independent lovely woman working right next to me
I guess thought she was too independent to love again
But we had a common thread in life which was we love people as they are
Soon we found that common thread was woven throughout our future life
As we touch we still honor our past lifelong partners but now each other.
My Dear I love you so much and I am still unable to show you my total self
I have found senior love can be as wonderful as young love because of you!

No 90

A MIRROR OF LOVE

When a lover looks into a mirror
What do they see?
In most cases it is the true reflection of that person
Still in a senior love affair it might be a dream of sorts
That is not the case between you and me
For what I see is a loving and true lady
Who has pretty hazel eyes that light up my heart
Who has a smile that lightens my daily worries
And a touch of an angel who protects me from evil
She is reflected in my mind each and every day
As my imagination of her is at play
No mirror could reflect my love back to me
For it can only be cast across space to her
Where can a senior love move forward with a mirror?
I guess only with her touch and maybe a soft tear.
She has a way with her hand brushing in my hair
Thus when she does it I have not a care
I am so lucky to have her come into my life so late in years
And with her daily touch I feel my heart shouting out cheers.
Not all senior lovers are so lucky as we two
But for us it is a rebirth which is between us becoming so true.
We have known true love in the past
God took away our partners so we thought our lives would crash.
But being a good God he gave us each other with a love that would last.
Our lips meet in a love which neither of us would have thought could ever happen
We enjoy our gift of love as we hold each other while others for us are clappin' .

No. 91

YOUR BARE TOUCH

Your touch slowly pushes across my bare scalp

And I cringe at the thought that it feels so wonderful.

I even feel guilty for I love it so much

For this isn't the way love should be

No, it must be more quiet and suggestive

But it isn't happening that way with you and me.

You touch me with that golden touch of a thousand years

That women have known how to make a man feel so helpless with their loving touch

And I find myself under that spell from the ages you bring to me

My head feels so relaxed and I can wonder if I escape the power of your hands

But can I say I am loving it and wanting you to stroke me all over

Still I feel a strong refrain within me being of very afraid.

I know I must not let myself go for I can hurt you in ways you don't know

I search for the loving answer to my fears

Yet I find none so I yield to you when you can still escape

My hair is thin on my old bean but it is still connected to my heart

And there you dance in my very being.

I only hope someday I have the courage to be the lover it seems you would like.

The mind is willing but the flesh is fumbling for the right answer.

I expect this might be the case in all senior loves

And I never thought in a million years to be caught up in one!

No 92

GOODNIGHT SWEETHEART

Goodnight Sweetheart parting is such sweet sorrow
Yet I know my love lingers in your heart until tomorrow.
I leave the touch of your lips dangling in our parting
And in my mind wild thoughts are starting.
You laughed a sweet girl smile at me as I acted stupid in my singing attempt
And you are even sweeter in my new songs for you I invent.
What has come over me as I glance back at you?
Your power of knowing me better than myself is so true.
I think I am so clever as I make a parting remark
But all that does is in my heart a longing start.
I say to myself I need time to be alone
Still that longing for you begins as I return home.
Where is that singing of love in my heart?
Does it hide until we touch again for it to start?
I see leaves and branches high in the trees dancing
Then I know as a senior love together we are chancing.
We are never sure of tomorrow in our life's plan
Still the overpowering love of you tells me I will be there if I can.
Goodnight Sweetheart as parting each time is not what we truly want
We need the touch of each other each day making our love so true that is what we
got.

No. 93

YOUR TOUCH HEALS MY HURT

Your touch makes my hurts go away
Your touch I yearn for each day.
The way you mess with my hair
From your touch I know how much for me you care.
I may be suffering from an unhappy event
Still with your touch away it went.
I feel your loving touch when I lie quietly on my bed
It is then I feel your touch moving slowly across my head.
I had thoughts that maybe it was like a mother's touch
And I again wanted to feel her touch on my head so much.
Your loving touch is not that but one of a lover reaching out
For another with the expression of love that is what it is about.
Our lips meet in the expression of our love for each other
Yet the loving touch of your hands running through my hair is that of a lover.
The chills down the back of my neck on to my arms
Makes for a love expression that you turn into a loving charm.
Your touch quickly heals any of my wounds I may have
For the magic of your fingers drives out any pain plus all that is bad.
I wish my touch would do the same to you
For I know how our love for each other is so true.
We now have each other with whom we can share our hurts in life
And that is what a true love between a woman and man is so nice.

No. 94

THOUGHTS IN FLIGHT

As my thoughts take flight
In the middle of the night.
My mind looks around for you
Then in a sleepless fog you walk through.
We join hands as we walk along in my dream
As we are blended into one it seems.
Your smile expresses in my dream a deep and passionate love
And I want to awake to really hold you at this time when I am given a shove.
My pillow allows me no escape at that moment
As I watch you drift away from my arms then I feel helpless.
I reach out to pull you back
As my hands bang into the cupboards above my bed
When suddenly I feel an empty feeling as my arms drop to my sides
So my mind realizes too many times awake my love for you I hide.
I wish only to kiss you in secret places only lovers know
And how many times my deep love for you I fail to show.
Again my thoughts take flight
On this sleepless night.
It is getting nearer to the time I must no longer dream
Instead to you I must show you my deep love it seems.

No. 95

HOW CAN YOU LOVE AGAIN

How can you love again?
Where has your love been?
One asks these questions after the death of their lifelong partner
And the answer isn't easy, as death has pulled their thoughts apart.
Still when the right two are matched in love
One must consider it happens because of a push from above.
You can love again I have found
For there the new love was on this second go around.
You were there all the time
And I had to look elsewhere before you were my greatest find.
Your first kiss and touch made me feel alive again
Your hazel eyes pushed aside my fears and a loving flame it fanned.
I knew once I found you a person could love for a second time
Plus it would be with family, relatives and friends just fine.
We kinda dance and sway when we hold each other in a hug
It is then at my heartstrings you do tug.
What would life be like without you I wonder?
So I don't even consider the answer as I enjoy your splendor
I am so glad you came into my life to lift my spirits up
Plus you filled my life as only you could like an overflowing cup.
God is good
God is great for He joined us as I knew he would.

No. 96

YOU ARE ONE IN A MILLION

Darling, I think of the first day when you crossed my trail
For you see I never walk a path that is straight.
You have been a very true friend
And my Thanksgiving wish is for you to be
Always present in my life as we travel toward the end.
I know that is far off, while we walk or ride our bikes
Yet feeling we could at any time do it together.
You with your life and me with mine at times
Do travel a different trail but each of us knows the other is close by.
You have a great day and many more along the days ahead.

No. 97

MY LIGHT

Darling, you are the light of my life
And that makes each day so nice.
Each waking moment I find you an important light
That shines as a beacon guiding me each day and night.
In my silent and working times I still have you in my mind
And that is just great better than just fine!
I know you get upset with my trying to do too much for you
But that is what keeps me going and away from being blue.
You do so much with your infectious smile
And I carry it in my heart plus in my writing style.
I am so thankful this Thanksgiving Day
That into my life with your heart you came to stay.
Many more days we will share
Still never having any time to spare.
Bless you for being you and such a great friend
And that our love continues to the world's end.

No. 98

ONE MORE YEAR

My Darling, now that you are over the hump of 39
You can relax for the rest of life is all downhill
Still the ride is the most fun
For you have commanded the many skills to live happily.
Remember how we thought when we first met
It was sort of the midwest meeting the east coast
Where I thought all of you talked funny
But I discovered with your love we speak the same language
Your birthday is very important to me
For you are part of my life till death do us part.
Holding your hand as we walk sends a secret electric spark
Up my arm and into my heart telling of your love
And the return message to your heart is "I love you more each day!"
So with this birthday I find myself enjoying it more than anything
I have in years.
HAPPY BIRTHDAY MY LOVE!!!!

No 99

A QUICK THOUGHT OR TWO

Where am I if I am with you?
Do we make a wonderful couple us two?
Why do we think so much alike?
Is it okay for a woman and man to do this or isn't it right?
Where can I go if not with you to have fun?
Would it be the same as jogging in the sun?
Why would anyone ask such foolish questions?
Is it because on her I am trying to make an impression?
Why should she love me so much?
Why don't I have a clue or even the slightest hunch?
Does she like the silly things I say?
Can she possibly put up with me another day?
Why do we enjoy each other all the time?
What I love most is she puts up with me just fine
Why do I ask all these silly questions when I know?
Hand and hand we together will travel this land
Enjoying each other as best we can!

No. 100

WALK HAND AND HAND WITH ME

Darling, you and I walk hand and hand
Dealing with life the best we can.
I know at times you get so frustrated with me
This I know from the unhappy look in your eyes but this is the way I be.
We sit across from each other in our special coffee place
As we look longingly into the other's face.
We have our own way to drink our coffee sitting there
I know for each other we desperately care.
What more in life is there but drinking coffee each day
It is our thing as others may think it is a strange way.
We walk and talk as we go hand and hand
I believe we think of each other as being grand.
Why I act distant at the wrong times
Is my dinger can ring my chimes.
I try to be bold to think all is okay
Still I know what should be doesn't happen that way.
Still I want you to bear up, walk hand and hand with me
You are my dream in life now
So you will learn to put up with me somehow.

No. 101

AS THE BREEZE FLOWS

Across the wide pasture field a gentle breeze flows
Lifting up a couples spirits and love as it goes.
We look at each other with beckoning eyes
As we hug each other pushing our feeling on high.
You stroke my hair as gentle as you did your first born
Thus it is a sensation within me building to a storm.
I feel your genuine heart reaching out to touch mine
Our thoughts mash together with emotions about to grind.
Yes, the breeze flows gently across the field
And from you another kiss I am about to steal.
A mischief dances in your eyes as I look deeply into them
My thoughts are tossed about like in a whirling wind.
Again with your touch I feel the gentle breeze
Your fingers rubbing my back in a way to tease.
What makes you so enchanting to me?
Could it be as we stand side by side that gentle flowing breeze?
The softness of your touch affects me as you do tease
And it all happens hugging each other in that gentle breeze.

No. 102

TAKE US AS WE ARE

Take us as we are or let us go
Let our love move along somewhat slow.
You peck a little kiss on my neck
My heart asks what is next?
I search my thoughts trying to find an honest answer
But I find there is none in love or with a belly dancer.
I am not sure my thoughts are on target now
But I am trying to say "I love you" somehow.
What is a poor fellow to do in old age,
You surely can't let your blood pressure surge and rage.
You can attempt to pull the straps over tight on your shoes
As an old senior guy for your life you have already paid your dues.
This lovely lady who has come into your life
Is really wonderful, lovely, genuine and super nice.
You don't really know how to act
Plus what was it you did for her to attract.
I love her dearly and give up on asking why
I just know she is the apple of my eye.

No. 103

WHERE DO YOU GO?

There the two of us were sitting in an adventure show
When suddenly I was embarrassed I had to go.
My new lovely lady might not understand
That suddenly I had to go to the can!
We had not dated much before
So I didn't want to be a bore.
One good thing we both had lost our partners of life
And just maybe she could understand a man which would be nice.
Still like a school boy on the first date
I attempted to hold and dreading my fate.
I was about to burst at the seams
She suggested I get up and go before I wet my jeans.
What a woman who read my mind!
After that I knew in my heart she was my kind!

No 104

APPLE OF THE EYE

Love is in the eye of the beholder.
The heart beats faster,
With no scientific reason in sight.
One swallows down the lump in the throat,
Never knowing what has happened.
It may be love at first sight or a long growing one,
But one knows the same time as the other.
Could it be the apple of the eye,
Or just a happiness that will last a lifetime?
What does an apple have to do with love, you ask?
Just remember what happened to Adam and Eve!

No. 105

HARKEN OUR HEARTS

All our ancestors speak to us at times,
We fear what they say yet we must listen.
Like it or not we walk in their light and ways,
We do it each and every day.
We are a sum total of our ancestral past.
Even though we add to the history line,
We will pass most of it on to our children in time.
Death robs us of a loved one when they are in full bloom,
It leaves their space, ways and an empty room.
What God whispers if we will shut up and listen,
In the wind, trees and quiet He gives a message.
"My love, I love you.
If you will go within yourself,
You will see I have given you a special angel of your own.
Feel that your angel standing with you in all you do.
When you are wrong the angel will guide you back to right,
And in your happiness and celebration the angel will join in.
I love you, my love,
But you must search, feel and listen to me once in a while,
For I send you the angel to be my guide to you in life's style.
Are you so blind you can't see your angel standing next to you?
No matter, my love, I will still love you in all you do."
Harken my heart, I hear you O'Lord and I believe,
Our personal angel from you we do receive.
We will listen and follow your ways,
Through the rest of our days.

No. 106

A Little Bird Told Us So

Love on First Sight
A Little Bird Told Us So
We gaze into each other's eyes,
We see only love and clear blue skies.
What was the attraction that brought us to each other?
We doubt if it was any one thing,
But when near each other our hearts' together still sing.
Our love has deepened with time which was started a long time ago,
All because to each of us, a little bird told us so.

No. 107

TO GIVE UP THE GHOST

I gave up the ghost
When I passed your way.
My heart stopped
My eyes popped.
Where have you been all my life?
I must have died and gone to heaven.
Your beauty can't be expressed in a few words,
First love is like this, I have heard.
My emotions I must put on hold,
And my feeling for you will never to anyone be told.
You walked into my life forever and so did love,
For an air terminal is no place for love between a duck and a dove.

No. 108

WHERE ARE WE?

If we walked across this land,
Would we be hand in hand?
Would we see all about,
And would we whisper or shout?
Love is a mystery in life,
It can cause happiness or strife.
I don't know how you feel,
But my heart is up for grabs.
Please don't break it as it is not made of steel,
And don't feed me love in bits and dabs.
Walk with me in truth and love,
For our love can only be embraced from up above.

No. 109

LOVE IS A SPLENDID THING

Love comes in any style,
Between parents and a child,
Young couples for each other,
Yes, especially for young lovers.
What a sickness over them will fall,
They spat and let it be unsolved enough to make one bawl.
They at that time are afraid to each other hold,
When fears and hates go untold.
Does this make love grow deeper?
Or is it a way out that is really cheaper.
A true love will stand any strain,
A loving heart can bear any pain.
All loves are rocky for the brave,
But a true love goes on until the grave.
All true loves are worth enough to save,
Providing both partners came and gave.
Remember our backgrounds are not the same,
Until we came together we each played a different game.
You know how when things are wrong,
Each of you know-no matter what-for the other you long.
Advice comes in all forms,
But yet real love will weather all storms.
Give, take and be honest with your mate,
I tell you then your love will be just great.

No. 110

I SEE IT IN YOUR EYES

I have found over time something quite mystic about you
Your eyes give you away when we are close and being so true.
You could not lie to me while looking me in the eye
No matter how hard you might try.
I only hope the same is true about me
For with your love I feel so untroubled and free.
I would hope I never lie to you about anything
Unless it would be to protect you from something.
Even then I doubt if I would
For the honesty between us is loving and good.
I feel we have come far enough to stand any disaster in our lives
So why lie to each other for together we might better cry.
It is a simple thing in a relationship I know
But so many lovers never really get the trust or even faith on which to go.
I am so happy you are one in a million and so important in my life
I want you to know having you touch me mentally and physically is really loving
and nice.

No. 111

WHY BABY WHY?

Why baby why?
Will come crawling across my mind until I die?
If we were younger it would race
But at our advanced age I am lucky to even have a trace.
When I hold you in my arms I feel like the first love
But then I go home after our last kiss and wonder were you a passing dove?
I float along in the sky and wonder why?
I know I am not superman but you make me feel like I can fly.
I move through each day like a zombie on a mission of love
But I don't suppose a zombie is like any love dove.
I walk in a line but still I stagger like a drunk with your love
Could God approve of my desires from above?
What is the matter with my vision and good senses?
Do you mess with my mind that much that I should sit on park benches?
I have even after leaving you flapped my arms in an attempt to fly
But found that isn't going to happen so disappointed I give up and do not cry.
Where is the justice in this hopeless feeling I have come over me?
You are not to blame for it is my stupid feelings running wild you see!
When I can be what you want me to be
Then from these little dreams each night I will be set free.

No. 112

WHAT IS IT?

I find myself wanting to write something special for you
But it seems it is held inside unable for me to express my feelings true.
I watch the great lovers of all time on TV
But they never say what I feel between you and me.
I watch you looking at me
And I feel so helpless yet my thoughts run free.
You have a power over me that I have never experienced in my life
I must admit if you use it right over me it is really nice.
I respect your opinion and important thoughts
Still I know those great expressions could never be bought.
Your hand in my hair is not fair
It makes my thoughts of what is important not really care.
You have an influence over me which I think might be okay
But if I didn't I would not let it stay.
You are so honest in your love I hope I am able to return it right
I am sorry I can not express it when we are together at night.
It seems I stumble around like a new lover which I am not.
What happens between us most each of us have forgot.
I enjoy our touching and being together a lot
But what else I must admit in love I have not.
I hope in our love we can be just special friends of sorts
I have nothing anyone would want even in sports.
So I love you in a special way
I love you each and every day.
This may not be the love you had hoped for
But I am at the present giving you love and nothing more.

No. 113

AS ONE

My love came across your path a while ago
For the most part since then together we go.
I find myself wondering what you need in your life
I mean besides my love for you, which makes my life so nice.
You have taken my scribbling of thoughts and words on paper
You turned them into useful thoughts and meaningful words in all my capers.
You have a loving touch in you, which you are able to apply to me
Thus my writings become inspiring enough that my thoughts are free.
Your loving touch when you brush your hand in my hair
Alights a longing in me that takes my mind and writing everywhere.
My love and concern for you being happy in life each day and night
I at times believe you as my damsel in distress and my being the saving knight.
I could go on at length
But instead I lend you my love and inner strength.

No. 114

HOW I KNOW

How do I know for me you care?
Maybe it is the way you run your fingers through my sparse hair
I wonder why your fingers play in my thinning hair up there?
Yet I don't want to really know only for you I do care.
As we wander out on our many little driving trips
With your hand playing all worries from my mind slips.
You look into my eyes with such loving tenderness
Just to have you close to me I know I am blessed.
We kid about the lottery and what we would do should we win
I guess we both feel that with each other we share it mostly with friends and kin.
When we kiss I feel you are the most important person on earth
Thus being apart at times makes my heart longing for you even worse.
Rain clouds gather in the distant sky
And the birds soar on the wind currents ever so high.
I wonder then if they can see our spirits flowing by
So if God blessed our love then why can't our spirits together fly?
I know that many seniors never get to know or have a love like ours
Instead they cling to the past for hundreds of hours.
We have not put aside our past
We just don't live it for each day together we want to last.
I am not a very good dancer this I want you to know
But with the modern dancing for your love I could put on a real fantastoc show
You make my mind come alive with your devotional love
It writes about my past, present and future planned from above.
My wit is driven by your laughter at times
Some of which would put me in trouble with the law as a crime.
You set me off like a little boy showing off for a little girl
I try to attract you with my antics and my golden boy's curls.

Why I do this I am not sure
But with each of your stares a kiss is the necessary cure.
Yes, my love! I know I need your love
And I think you need mine just because!

No. 115

LOVE WITH ALL WE GOT

You and I share our love with each touch
I love you and you love me maybe too much?
I think not!
We each love the other with all we got.
We dine out when we can afford it
But mainly we eat out of our cupboard and at the kitchen table we sit.
A love at the senior level is a little different than in our youth
Our expressions of love are sincere truth.
We don't try to fool each other with a love game
For we know full well time is against us in life's moving train.
We touch each other with such a loving caress
You rub your hand across my balding head leaving those few hairs in a mess.
We hold hands the moment from our car we alight
Sometimes squeezing light and other times holding hands so tight.
Our eyes meet from time to time as we sip our coffee each day
And somehow our minds toward each other are at play.
Our children are grown but they don't pull us apart
They all think for us staying together is smart.
We both enjoy those little drives in day or in the moonlight
Never knowing for sure where we are going yet being together is just right.
Our future is unknown as it is true for seniors like us
Things that use to bother us in youth now over them we don't fuss.
We get tickled when I stare at something while driving
I drift out of the beaten path as you warn me before under the dash you might be diving.
We both think about how we came to be such great friends and in love
Yet we never speak of the time it might end when we are called by God above.

No. 116

HAVE YOU EVER THOUGHT?

Terri you and I are lucky
You came uncertain of whether to come or not
You found Rick who was searching too
Your search ended happily.
It was here where I lost my wife after years of pain
And I made a big mistake as another appeared
But it was wrong.
I finally saw another who was alone
Who turned my life around by just being herself
She encouraged me when all others just smiled at my efforts
She saw a strength in me I had not called on in a long time
She was quiet but determined to see me as I was.
You, Terri, found the same in Rick
I do not know if it was you or he that needed your silent strength
But I am betting it was Rick like me who needed you.
Why I ask myself is it men who fumble around in the darkest of life
And it is a woman put on earth by God who finds that wandering soul
Then silently grabs the man by the nose and leads him back to himself.
Is that what God intended the woman to do for most men?
I think not but I am so happy that God cared enough about me
He put a special person which happens to be a woman
In my life to lead me to the riches of life
Still she goes along for my over-active pride and ego
Making sure I don't falter or stray as I have done in the past.
Thank you, God!!

No. 117

CRASH COURSE ON LOVE AGAIN

Look up my pant leg you devil
You had better keep you mind of a clean level.
Look down my blouse you naughty man
I have covered all I can
Make our hearts race toward each other
You and I would make good lovers.
You seem to lean out of that cold cream ad
And about you I am loving you like mad.
I know you as a more loving person than you try to appear
Never could away from you my love steer.
I find you a strong woman who I need at this point in my life
I still try to be that young lover of the past being not so nice.
When I think of a new senior love I feel I am on a crash course in love
But then again as I look at the Bible I know this love comes from above.
My heart races as our hands touch
I guess I must admit I love you so much.
What could a marriage counselor tell an old goat like me?
Could they say I must progress slower in my love for you and not be a big tease?
Should I have a lifetime ahead of me that might be okay?
But at my age I must rush ahead with my love for you each day.
When I am away from you this you don't know
I take a deep breath just to keep on my love path and go a little slow.
I have been terrible at passion all of my life
And to think I get a chance to love two superior women in a lifetime is super nice.
I know we don't do all the foolish things we did when we were young
It is a deeper love I feel in my heart is being sung.
I notice more things about you than I would have in younger days
Your wreckless brushing of your hand over my thinning hair on my mind plays.

Your understanding of when I am silent or just staring into space
And the words you speak then as you softly look into my face.
It seems that with you I can speak words of love without saying a thing
Which you know as you answer back makes my heart sing.
I am so lucky to have you in my life as a senior love after stumbling around
So each day I am taking a crash course on love I have now found

No. 118

BITE MY LIP

I think of you when all is quiet and I am alone
What are you doing in your home.
As a senior of some years
I wonder if I can hold you today so near.
Could you be thinking of me?
Or are you thinking it is good to be single and free?
Could you be dreaming about when you were young?
And now again that freedom has begun.
Is it so precious that you are alone and doing things your way
Or do you wish you had again a partner with whom to play?
Just to take simple drives around the neighborhood in the afternoon
Or someone with whom you could again talk under a harvest moon?
I wonder what I am thinking if it is the same as you?
Love words dance in my head but will not come out
My heart casts them out to you with a shout.
A ringing in my ears is caused when you are near
My arms and hands become playful longing for you, dear.
I bite my lip as I have much to say
Some I could mumble and some for another day.
Why I would not say all in these senior years?
I guess it is caused by my stupid manly fears.
Life is getting so short
Maybe I should quit the lip biting and not give a snort!
I think of you and your importance in my life
I not only think of you "My Love" once a day but twice.
For the remainder of our lives may we travel down the same path
May our love for each other to the end last.

My hope is we continue to share life's pleasures together
And may our love for each other continue on forever.

No. 119

GOODNIGHT MY DEAR

Yes, I say goodnight my dear
As I see you my dreams O'so clear.
You are standing there ever so beautiful in summer shorts
And my heart skips a beat, I paw the ground and my nose kind of snorts.
I am not a bull at heart
But being with you each time makes my day start.
I wonder many times a day when I write
Where would I have been if you had been there for me day and night?
Each time we part into our nightly worlds
Your laughter each time haunts me into wanting to dive into the ocean searching
for pearls.
I would then string them with love to give to you at morning light
But being an old senior person of some good sense I will just kiss you goodnight.
I trick myself into believing again as a youth I might do crazy love things for you
But each time I drive my body to do them I find it can't follow through.
You say you will take me the way I am
Still I want to give you more of my love than I can.
I would swim the deepest river for you my dear!
And climb the highest mountain but I know I would never the peak clear.
You still say don't drive myself into trying something I can't do
And I know you don't expect me to.
I am an old senior man with a twinkle in my eye
But much of my body functions have said "Bye! Bye!"
Why a lovely senior lady like you
Would want an old senior man like me it must be senior love so true?
I write to you verse after verse
It is your understanding, support and love that has put on me this curse!
I never knew a love like I have for you

I call it a senior love without having a nurse.

I write with my heart saying things deep within me

For at senior age my spirit of love has been set free.

When your hand touches my mine

All my fears of life and death seem set aside and all the world is just fine.

I know we are much of the time now apart

But I know we need separation to create a longing in our heart.

You have many things you like personally to do

And I have those same dumb practices that make my day go through.

After all those years we lived with our partners of the past

We still have great memories that in silence and alone we want to last.

Yes, you gave me back a love and life I thought was lost

And quietly you give me the love in your heart at no cost.

We enjoy many things in life yet we are like newlyweds of the past

I want this special love until our deaths to last.

I probably would not be alive today if you didn't warn me about a stop light or two

Had you not been with me I would have crashed when ignoring them I raced through.

I am not saying that is a cause of being a senior person now

I just forget those silly stop lights flashing on somehow.

We are able to talk about our past loves without concern

For we are proud of our past partners and a love for them still in our hearts burn.

We are on a life's long dream of living on without any great fuss

We don't even wonder each day together how long it will be for us.

We live each day with a love different when in our youth

And we don't need when we kiss a kissing booth.

We can do it out in the open no matter what others might say,

For we are loving and living together each day.

So should the writing of this poem light a fire under you and yours

Now as senior lovers when we kiss each other we don't have to keep score.

When one of us comes up lame and has to have a hospital stay

The other pitches in to help but mainly ask God for help as we pray.

It seems many times one of us has all sorts of problems at hand
But isn't it great to have a pal, lover and friend with you stand.
One never dreams in our youth of these struggles in senior life
Still we are so thankful to the Lord we don't have to go through it twice.
Friends rally around us when we are in need
And when they are struggling we rush to return their good deed.
So Darling let's waltz around the floor just once more
Because no matter what we do our bodies will always be a little sore.

No. 120

RUN FOR COVER

I question a new senior love from the start
Should I and all the reasons don't seem too smart?
Am I too old to really make love?
I guess that will have to be answered by God above.
I still have young ideas dancing in my head
And I looked into the mirror—No! I am not dead.
I know for sure the back seat of car is not the right place
But I will clear the junk out of there just in case.
As we talk about our partners of the past
I think maybe she has me outclassed.
Is it possible the love we are now having
Just might be deeper in spirit so I should quit crabbing?
I know my sexual drive and that wild look in my eyes has crept way
Still the idea dances in my head as with words we now play.
Where has all the love play craziness gone?
I guess like in that TV game I have been "Gonged!"
She is just a real looker these days of senior desire
And to make her happy sets my thoughts on fire.
Where have all the little tricks of love making gone?
I now realize they were just in some dumb old song.
We hold hands as much as we can everywhere we go
But that only speeds up the heartbeat to fast from slow.

No. 121

A TOSSED SALAD

I feel like a tossed salad at times
My feelings of past loyalty to my mate of the past is a crime.
She lived a wonderful life of happiness and sadness as one does
And she fought a fantastic battle to her death just because.
I loved her as a mate of 40 plus years as the living partner does
She suffered more from my goofs over the years just because.
As I look back I didn't mean to hurt at anytime
Still many of my goofs happened at the wrong time;
Like any remaining mate I wonder what I could have done different in her life
And no matter what I think I loved her totally and the memories are still nice.
I knew my life must go on no matter what
I finally found another in the same situation who filled that loving spot.
We blended in a unknown love that only a senior person might know
For in our lives it made happiness and whole beautiful show.
We began to hold hands like a couple of kids of the past
And we knew it would never end until death comes at last.
We started attending a church to fulfill a longing in each
For again in God's way we had to again stretch out our arms to HIM reach.
We knew we could never re-capture our youth
But as a senior lover it is hard to accept the truth.
We walk together on our way to daily coffee breaks
For in our thinking that is what to be together in love it takes.
I wonder about her love for a partner of second choice
I wish to God that I had for her been first.
Her children must think we are crazy in a way
And my gang thinks she is great for keeping me off them each day.
I toss away my thoughts of the past when I am with her
I hope she does the same but I bet her past husband does at times concur.

How could one toss out all those wonder years of the past?
We are surprised as we live on and they didn't last.
As a senior lover it is okay to love again
For a senior person this is a recycling land.
I am so glad my God cared about me enough to send into my life a saint
For she got a man who is really not one who ain't.
My new lover lit a flame under my butt that is truth
I have done many things that now she is going to make me see through.
God! What do you have in mind for me?
Will I write more words that will please you or will they fly away being set free
I hang on her every word of suggestion each time and day
For she has a way of saying them in an important way.

No. 122

LIGHTNING FOR MY LOVE

My honey has been hit by lightning
Oh! I think that is frightening!
Then those long hours in the hospital for her
What was wrong with her to the doctor it never occurred.
She had hurried out to correct the awning
A severe storm was just spawning.
There was a strike of lightning near by
And streaks of current from it were sent out on the fly.
As my love had her right hand on the alummun brace
A bolt struck her and for a time her memory was lost without a trace.
Some friends found her standing there with that memory lost
They got her inside then attempted to get her mind uncrossed.
I arrived on the scene, as a lover should do
My love spent five days in that hospital before all was through.
She then returned to us with all very happy she was alive
Seeing she was somewhat healthy and in good spirits jokes began to fly.
For my love I was probably the worst tease
But she took all the jokes about being a lightning rod with ease.
No matter what we teased her about she knew we loved her with all our hearts
For sure when another storm comes about she'll be inside before the lightning
starts.

No. 123

EATING OUT

The way of love with our senior life
It's eating out and eating what we want then pay the price.
Holding hands with you beneath the table is fun
It like our first loves when we were young.
Now again we as senior lovers forgetting our past
Not cooking or dishes to do we are freed at last.
As you and I come from different eating habits
By eating out we can get the food we like to help swallow down our different tablets.
Speaking of medicine that too is another reason for eating out
It is then we can take the twenty some different pills not caring what each is about.
We have them with our eggs and toast
Or work them in with the gravy and pork roast.
Whether the pills are to be taken early or late
Eating at a restaurant other seniors just smile knowing our eternal fate.
I love the idea each time I will not have to do the dishes which I hate
But on the other hand within an hour after I am not sure what I ate.
It is so romantic being with you at some fantastic restaurant like Burger King
Just knowing the meal will be good and cheap makes my heart sing.
Where does all the time go when you are at a buffet at a Chinese diner?
For as I stuff my face and you eat lightly I can think of nothing finer.
I guess the most fun is trying to agree on which restaurant tonight
In the senior years it doesn't end up in a fight.
I try to impress you at meal time with my proper manners
It is not the eating out but our love for each other that matters.
You are so proper in your table manners and I am such a clutch
But that really doesn't bother either of us for we love each other so much.
I hate to bring this up but eating out so much can cause a problem of sorts

I never know in these senior years whether I have to dress properly or just come in shorts.

The restaurants that we try that are new or just our regular haunts

We have to watch our weight for into overweight we don't want to launch.

Yes, eating out in the senior years is great

But most of all it is having a meal with you as my special date.

No. 124

PILLOW TALK

I lie in bed at night hugging my pillow
Thinking of you and wishing you were beside me.
I dream of having your arms around me
Sheltering me within their circle of love,
Wanting only to feel your body curled around mine,
Your breath on my cheek, my lips remembering the warmth of your kisses,
But the pillow next to mine is empty.
I listen for whispers in the night that do not come,
Needing the tender touches telling me of your love.
Wanting so desperately to show my love for you,
To feel the silk of your skin beneath my hands,
My thoughts reach out to you sending my messages of love.
I pray to God each night telling Him of my love for you,
Asking Him to watch over you and guide you safely through the night.
The time remaining to us grows shorter with each passing day
Will we ever overcome our fears and shyness?

No. 125

SPARKY

You were indirectly struck by a lightning bolt
And for a short period of time your mind was afloat.
You were one lucky gal
And you are so special to me not just a pal.
Seniors continue to love as any young person does
But now at our age holding hands gives us a buzz.
It was a terrible thing that happened to you
Plus you were lucky to remain alive, which is true.
What happened after you returned to your home?
Must tell you of your friends' love for you now that you no longer roam.
Some of the humor has replaced the seriousness of the event
And the nicknames you have been assigned have come and went.
The nickname that seems to have stuck
Is "Sparky" like you had been racing along like a Mack truck.
I am not sure whether this nickname fits you right
Yet now when you kiss me my thoughts take flight.
Maybe "Sparky" is right for you in a way
For being near you now more than ever makes my day.
Your being in the hospital while doctors were trying to discover your plight
I went home to pray for your return each night.
We may not live like maybe we should
But again for both of us that might okay and good.
Too many times I find myself so set in my ways
I wonder if I might give you more pain on many days.
Still "Sparky" I love you and cherish all the time we are together
And hopefully with my foolish habits you will be able to weather.
There is no way I would be able to write a word if not away from you
For once away my love for you starts a pain or longing, which brings words so true.

So in silence "Sparky" my senior love, your secret nickname will remain hidden
And in time it will be lost and no longer will it be said or written.

No. 126

WHERE DO I START?

No man is good at love at least that is what I think
He opens his mouth with flowery words that stink.
How can I tell you how much you mean to me?
You touch me and I go wild and spirit free.
I know you have done this to another man
And I to another woman in my fumbling way as best I can.
Those were our partners of the past
And now we have a deep love that for eternity can last.
I never knew as a senior lover I could be so bold
I had heard of it for years but what really happens I was never told.
Our holding hands each time we are together as best we can
I feel a magic travel up my arm and it goes "Wham!"
Your eyes gazing at me as I drive along
I know you don't know that in my heart lights a mystic song.
I think you were raised millions of miles away from me
Yet here we are looking into each other's eyes any time we are free.
I wonder if we would have met in an earlier life
I doubt it for I think God planned it this way which is really nice.
We could have plodded along our lonely path determined by fate
Which we would have just thought God meant it for us yet we did hate!
I have wondered why we came together in mind and thought
At times I think maybe we had not been for that is the way I was taught.
At that time I feel your touch on my hand and I know all is all right
And how I want to crest you and hold you ever so tight.
You have become my soul and heart in my mind
You are the guiding light which every lost soul especially a lost man needs
On your strength I desperately feed.
As I walk along any lonely path in a small patch of woods

I know whatever you do for me be it suggestions or your touch is good.

I walk in the darkness of life and you are the light

You turn each of my days from despair to right.

I know God wanted me to something important in life

But with you at my side I know it will be right and really nice.

I write this in the greatest thoughts of my life still I question why?

It must be God has more things to say through me which some times I don't buy.

Your hand brushing across my head just drives me wild

I know you are sure at that time I am your child.

I hope you never quit that silly habit as we drive along

For in my heart with your hand stroking away it sings a loving song.

I wonder if we could have given each other what we had

I think not for God planned it this way for good or bad.

We had our partners of love and for children we bore in life along

We were destine to meet late in life after our partners were gone.

God had other deep plans for us which are not truly clear

But I want you to know I love you so much my DEAR!

I can't give you back your youth or any past loves

I can only give you my pledge of love and faith which is approved from above.

When I hold you I feel safe and secure in this world

I know you are strength and love for me plus being a super undiscovered pearl.

Why God allowed me to enter your life after floundering around?

I will never know but so grateful I will always in life be bound.

Just your touch of love turned my life to new heights

And when I lie my head on my pillow at night I know because of you all is right.

I know you are unaware of the power you have with me

But I want you to know it is love deeper than I could ever believe.

I put on my socks in the morning light

And I think back when in my dreams you were with me last night.

I am so happy in my senior love on this day

For on my mind thoughts of you dance as two fawns at play.

This senior love of mine is overwhelming when I think of my desires for you

Still I can do nothing which would belittle you or me which is true.
I have found a love for your children even though grown
As I hear about them they are super together or alone.
Maybe someday soon I will meet them each whether by email or phone.
They will join in my heart as one of my own
Knowing their mother is never alone.
I love you my dear with your touching my hand or head
That is the way it will be until I am dead.

No. 127

APOLLO

Oh! Apollo the Greek, god of love
I am now asking to come down from above.
You were a great lover in the past
Now I want your help to say to my lover words that will last!
I search each time we are seated next to each other
I find my thoughts of love over her hover.
Why can't I commit myself totally to her?
I think it is our past lives to what I refer.
She came from a family of strict rules and such
I was raised loosely pretty much.
She had rules of life pressed on her in life
I had a free hand for making rules when needed which was nice.
She loves totally with every touch
I have become reserved in love pretty much.
I love her so deeply but can't bring myself to touch
She has come around to loving by giving of herself with one big punch.
I don't mean to hit me but that she loves as deeply as I
She just knows how to express it and I just let it fly by.
Apollo, how did you handle your loving women in the past?
And did your love for each other really last?
Apollo come with me to my next meeting with this lovely soul
Show me what I must do without being told.
I have fumbled badly in recent days
For I don't have your talent and loving ways.
I try to read how you handled the loves that last
But as I attempt them they just flounder around until they crash.
I need your secret ways that you used to win over so many maidens past
I can't play a lyre or any musical instrument if I could that would be a blast.

My lady of my dreams is with me always it seems
When I dream of love especially about her my heart for her screams.
Why sometimes I ask myself why did she come into my life when I was so messed
up
God saw my plight and He decided I was worth something so put love in my cup.
He took away the blindness in my eyes revealing her to me
And now Apollo, you have to show me how to love again properly.
She is so lovely even at this senior age
For me she is the mightiest lover I want to cage.

No. 128

THE SECOND TIME AROUND

When I am lonely and missing you
I read the beautiful poems you have written to me.
I think of when I knew I had fallen in love with you
How you seduced me with your soft brown eyes,
Your mouth and your hands sending exquisite shivers up my spine,
Long-dormant feelings coming to life, electrifying me.
Did you feel the ground shake beneath your feet?
Or was it only my foolish heart quaking?
Love the second time around is a wonderful gift,
A beautiful journey with your hand reaching out for mine,
Whispers on the wind carrying messages of love.
I have given you my heart—I am only yours,
Here to hold your hand, to love you and support you,
Your poetry sweet music to my soul.
The joy of being with you, of having you beside me brightens my life.
Your love sustains me as the sun nurtures the flowers.
When you look at me with love in your eyes,
A riot of impressions, erotic and exciting, race through me,
My love for you so intense.
I need your love, your kisses and your arms so strong around me.
Do you, too, hear the music of our spirits?

No. 129

LOOKING BACK

I was looking back to see
If you were looking at me.
I glance as I am driving to see you looking at me
I wonder what in the world in me you see?
I am so glad you can see some talent I might possess
I see your talent each and every day and that is why I love you I guess.
It is true your touch gives me a boost of energy each time we touch
I know that is another reason I love you so much.
Your stroking my few head hairs makes me curious in a way
Is your love pulling up from my brain my love thought of you on that day?
I could say it tickles as you run your hand across my head
It is then as I feel that love touch from you I know I am not dead.
I have never had anyone play with my hair
For it has for years been so scarce up there from the years of wear.
It sets off thoughts of what our love might have been
I was thinking of way back when.
Yes, I keep thinking what if with you and me
But if it had been would it today be setting dreams ever so free.
Sometimes I am thinking in these senior years
We no longer have those youthful fears.
It is a fact to us that we are nearing the end of life's trail
Still we can carry on, dreams or beautiful thoughts of each other in any plastic pail.
I find myself rambling when I am talking to you
Inside my love for you seems penned up that is true.
I am an old lover in my mind so why do I fumble for words
I am starting to realize the truth is I am more like one of those past nerds.
I am not sure what that means but it helps me to talk to myself about my love for
you

I know I was never one to express my true feelings of being blue.

I look into your eyes of love

And secretly thank all the angels, ancestors and God from above.

You have a way that I am sure you don't realize of a loving woman's power

For you have become a strength I need daily so I don't crawl into myself as a coward.

I am hoping I pass off a strength you might need each day of life

Just to know I might possess it makes the daily touching with you more than just nice.

I tried for a time to figure out how God nudged us together after my stupid mistakes

Then I found I really didn't care for He knew you had for me what it takes.

Your encouragement of my limited talent of writing was I am sure God sent

And when I doubted myself your strength and conviction for me you lent.

I never thought as a senior I would love so deeply as I now do

My dear, please love me until our lives are through.

Yes, as I look back over my life I find a mighty poor lover of sorts

But right now I feel like an old bull, pawing the dirt with my nostrils giving out snorts.

Don't laugh for it might be nice to have a male making a fool of himself over you

For I want most of all looking back and forward our love lives aren't through.

So my dear! Take this old foolish man as he is young in mind and an old body

I can't help it but I must finish this love message with be sure, he knows where is the potty.

No. 130

WHAT IF?

What if we had been neighbors of the past?
And our love for each other had on our lives a shadow cast.
That is not true as we came from different parts of the country
And now we are trying in the senior years to blend it comfortably.
You came from parents with a strong father image
And I came from a family of balance after an argument scrimmage.
We were so lucky to have wonderful marriage partners in life
That made our lives perfect for years of happy times and real nice.
We both came through the terrible suffering of our partners in later times
So we were somewhat caregivers in senior life which is just fine.
Does the care giving have an effect on our current love?
I think how could it for I floundered after the death of my partner dove.
I didn't know you when you were fighting a double battle of life
From experience I know that wasn't so nice.
I find you a challenging person of intrigue and mystery in a way
I really don't know you or your past except what little you tell or say.
I suppose you can read me like an open book as most women can
I know with your expert correcting of my writings I am like an opened can of
Spam.
I make a good meal if properly prepared in the way you might do
Still I think you are super and really cherish and love you.
I think how can a fool like me have the true love of a noble woman such as you are
Then when I hear you tell of your family I know apart we aren't very far.
Every time we walk together our hands meet
I have never held hands so much as with you and in senior years it is really neat.
I have traveled many miles in my work back in northwest Arkansas where people
are supreme

I rate you with them and that is a rating higher than "A" in anyone's book of super dreams.

I find I have a funny way of expressing my thoughts of love and honor

But "Darling" there is no one of whom I am fonder!

You know my dear I can never let anything finish without a smile

We go shopping at Wal Mart and you take quite a while.

That is perfectly okay for as a woman you need time to look and make sure

But "Honey!" the old men I have to wait with are not the type I need for a cure!

I must bring out of them all the thoughts of a lifetime.

That may be okay but while I wait on the bench for you hearing those stories is a crime.

I love going shopping with you once a week

For I know now I must sit to hear stories that are repeated never reaching a peak.

I think to myself "What if I didn't show?" for these old souls

I bet God would send me to hell to hear all those stories still untold!

I will wonder until God closes my eyes

What if we had met in youth would we have been together in future lives?

I think not for we were to grow in ways different yet blend into what we are today

I guess I must admit to myself I really like it that way.

I again wonder about our love now and in the past

"What if?" really doesn't matter I just want our present love for each other to last!

No. 131

LOVE IS WHERE YOU FIND IT

One can look high and low for love
It never appears until it is provided by our Lord from above.
A lady told many of a love for having a pet at home
She could come home late at night and not be alone.
A cowboy may be the distant lonesome sort of guy
We have heard that being said but it isn't the cows a ring he will buy.
One can look down a street at a neighbor who lives alone
Unless one of them wish a love for another the desire will just roam.
There are many kinds of love we are told
But the best one is when another person you can hold.
I am so glad my love you gave me an opening and chance
In the quiet of my home over your love I many times dance.
You study my face for some of my deepest thoughts
I try to hide them when in fact I hadn't ought
I don't want to be an open book for you in our love game
I want you to love me deeply but not like the ones of movie fame.
I really don't know what I want from your love
I am hoping maybe our Savior can tell me in case it comes to push or shove.
I think of your caring and touching me with your loving hand
I try to respond the best I can.
I think most of all it is your needing me some of the time
While all the times together for me you are so kind.
You are so independent at times it makes me admire you so much
Still I feel I am important to you in helping with chores but it is just a hunch.
You have a way of expressing yourself with those eyes of light brown or green
I guess the right color of them I am not sure it seems.
I have committed my life to you in most ways
Still I need the being alone on some days.

I am not sure you understand this crazy desire
But I think you need being alone for that is what for each other aspires.
We find each day new things and ways we are alike
So at times my defensive ways will leak like a defective dike.
Where our life paths come together is still in question
But many of our co-workers, family and friends have many suggestions.
I will honestly say I would have no recourse if we won that Florida lottery
But to suggest we share our lives, home and all of our Indian pottery.

No. 132

CAREGIVERS

To all who have to take care or have taken care of a spouse, parent or child
Who was sick, injured or even mentally crippled for a while.
This is a tribute to you for I have been there myself
It is a love deeper than marriage or for a child who is okay
It is a love which can never be expressed
Except in the giver's heart.
This special love carries you over all hardships
It gives you a new look at life as it is
Best of all it makes you a special person with love abounding.
As the Nordic folks of the legends remarked
You rise above yourself to be close to a god of the one you are caring for
May you never feel sorry for what you are doing
For God loves you more than anyone
For you are giving what He stands for in Heaven
You are a caregiver of another who can't provide for themselves.
May you stand high in your own mind
For those who admire you are supporting you just behind.
You have been given a task that most would shy or run from
But because you are strong, loving and caring you don't run.
You carry out each task easing the pain of your loved one
You will stay no matter what until God calls them or the battle is won.

No. 133

SOLITARY THOUGHTS

In the quiet hours of solitude
I think of you and how much I love you
Of how much I miss you when we are apart.
Your goodness and caring have hold of my heart,
Your beautiful smile and soft brown eyes draw me close.
I need your lips on mine, your arms around me
Would that we could be always together.
You need your time alone and I do understand-
Know that I am here when you need me.
Never did I think I would love again with such depth and intensity.
I try so hard not to overwhelm-
My hands aching to touch you, to show you my love.
You are my comfort, my strength, my best friend
But most of all you are the love of my life.

No. 134

YOUTH OF THE MIND

You dump some old Viagra pills down your toilet
You know what happened you didn't sit on it for four days.
You throw the empty pill box into the waste
What happened in there would make an FBI case?
They were out of date
For you knew when you bought them their fate.
You had dreamed about being a stud of sorts
But knew if you did you might land in court.
Dreams are wonderful when a man is alone
You just hoped knowing only in dreams Viagra makes you roam.
You are ashamed many times about your crazy thoughts of the past
For you thought sexual greatness would last.
Of course being somewhat normal you were never great
But in your mind you never dreamed of this fate.
You fumble around in your attempt to show you are the greatest
But your selection of being so is really tasteless.
You wonder if others as old as you
Have such dreams and lose them then become blue.
You know the other sex never has this trouble
But then a woman busted your imagine bubble.
A senior woman of your love held you close
You felt like a youngster about to again to roast.
Your mind whirled like when you were a pilot in the past
You knew this feeling of passionate love would not last.
You thought this is your only course as a senior lover now
You were already in the seniors junk pile this you couldn't allow.
You were so lucky your grandson said you are about the same
So you decided you were still in the love game.

You had put yourself down but you were not dead
You had plenty of loving and mischief ahead.
You lifted up your head and your heart for adventure
You were hoping to go out to love those senior women in your venture.
You are an animal in your mind of the worst kind
For you are a senior man on the prowl and some poor senior woman you will find.
Now wishing and bragging to yourself is fun
But when it comes at your age it never gets done.
You guess all the jokes you have heard about a senior man in the past
Must be true but with luck they cross your mind very fast.
Each day you thank God for allowing these youthful thoughts in your head
For that way you are sure you are not dead.
You can not be sure what at this age a woman might be thinking about a love
But no matter what it might be you are helpless without her loving shove.
You never in your younger days thought this might happen to me
As you listened to the older men tell what it took for them to make love or even
to tease.
Well it is true most of what you heard or was told
Your thoughts may remain about love but your body just got old.
So never give up your dreams or the ship
Because you mind is strong but your body did slip.

No. 135

FOOLING AROUND

I love fooling around with words
I guess because I love being among nerds.
I really don't know what a nerd is
I heard the word tossed around while watching a show on show biz.
I love living about as normal as an old man can be
I just don't enjoy sitting around instead my spirit runs free.
I have the crazy dreams of the past in my life which aren't always true
Still most of them lately are of you.
I place you back when you were young
I see you as a beautiful young one who was a little high strung.
As you say you were daddy's girl in many ways
And being with him were some of your glorious days.
I can see you now being that little tease
As now you do it to me with the greatest ease.
I know you learned most of it along life's trail
And I love you for it knowing you aren't in spirit frail.
You are such a strong person I find myself drawing on it
Many times a day when I find myself weakening wanting to run or just sit.
You are a spirit who demands only strength when the body fails
I am just beginning to find this happening to me but you lead me down the
winning trail.
When my body cries out "I hurt and I must retreat!"
You stand before me in strength ever so neat.
I wonder why God allowed you to love me when I nearly turned away
I now thank Him for you every day.
I bet many old men find themselves wandering in life
They have lost their partner of a lifetime which isn't so nice.
They are so dependent on that partner but not willing to admit it

So they make many mistakes before they look deep into themselves and just sit.

I had the great luck having God guide you into my life when all was lost

It may have been your interest in my writing but together we were tossed.

I wonder each day why you think I am interesting or even the one for you

But I am not questioning your judgment or your poor judgment I hope your love is true.

When you look at me with those hazy eyes I feel my soul, heart and blood pressure rise

I would have never been able to write any of these love notes without those eyes.

I am sure now we will walk through the rest of life together in some manner

I am afraid of hurting you by being with you all the time so I hide my battle banner.

Why can a man write to his lover on this clear blue sky day?

I guess God made it that way.

I wish I could take you into my arms right now

But I would fumble around not knowing just how

I guess God wanted lovers at our age to wander around a while to be sure

Maybe you aren't so confused as me but I am sure my love for you is pure.

I think back to my first kiss with a girl up in a hayloft back when

That wasn't the same I felt with you as I wanted to kiss you again and again!

I wonder if time had made the kiss better or was it you

Without question I knew the answer in a moment before we were through!!

You rang my bell as it hadn't rung in years

I guess maybe because of all those failures and tears.

I know you lost your partner along the way

And to think we found each other one day.

Your hand rubbing on my few head hairs in so super of course

I might use some super hair restorer even get some from a horse.

I question myself for writing you this love poem

I know the answer for you are in my heart and at my home.

We live each a different course which I am not sure is right

For we split and are separate each night.

I know it is my choice right now

But I wonder how you feel about it somehow.
I am afraid together we might drift apart
And with another as lovely as you I couldn't start.
Why does an old man like me write just a poem of love?
I guess God tells him to from his Heaven above
Each one is written in the deepest love.
Maybe each of us old folks needs a hand on us and a shove
For if God says so, "We better get with it and love!!"

No. 136

MY DEAR LOVE

I think back to when I was first attracted to you.

You had lost your lovely lifetime partner;

In your grief another took advantage of you.

When you were hurt my heart went out to you.

That you cared enough for another to marry was a pain I tried to ignore.

In time I got to know a lovely, sensitive and caring man.

When you shared your poetry with me you honored me.

I discovered a man ready to embrace life again,

With a sparkling wit and a huge capacity for love.

In my later years I have found love once more.

God has blessed me with a reason to live again;

A second chance at happiness is ours.

Even though we each enjoy some solitary time,

When we go to our separate homes I am sad.

I am ready to love again, afraid you don't want me.

Your poetry tells me otherwise and I am willing to wait.

Our playful teasing and loving leaves me shaken.

It would be enough just to have you hold me close at night,

Letting my caresses show my love for you.

I love you with a depth and intensity that is overwhelming.

Without you there would be no life.

My heart is in my throat as I send this to you.

I have bared my soul and I can only hope that you treat it kindly.

I love you

No. 137

FIRECRACKER LOVE

I am a little firecracker in love with you
When we kiss my heart nearly pops in tide
Your lips pressed against mine
I want to kiss you anytime.
Your arms around me light a flame
Arousing emotions I have trouble to tame.
Yes, I am a firecracker who around you is ready to pop
When you rub your hand across my head I whisper, "Don't stop!"
The field of hair on my old head may be sparse
But my love for you is no farce.
Without your love daily I walk through the valley of death
Yet I know losing you a fact of life I think about and dread.
I look forward to when we get a chance to work together at any time
You make any job a joy for being with you I can sneak a kiss which makes it fine.
I watch you walk going and coming from me
I can tell in your heart the spirit of life is being set free.
Yes, you are my firecracker of life
Kissing you once, "No!" I want to kiss you twice.
My firecracker fuse is lit by being with you
So with this poem I want you to know my firecracker love is true.

No. 138

YOUR HAND IN MINE

I walk with your hand in mine
I find I reach for your hand of love most of the time.
We alight from the car
I have your hand before we walk too far.
What is it with the hand holding at our age?
I can remember in our youth it was the youth's rage.
We are still carrying on the practice of tender love
I am sure there are many watching us from above.
I think that is great for I know they approve of our hand holding
If they didn't I am sure in some way they would of us be scolding.
I wonder many times was it fate who pulled us together now
Or is was our past that did it somehow?
I think at times I really do not know the true person you are
But as I think back to my partner of forty years or more were we really on par?
I wonder if that is the real way God wanted it in this world
He decided there must be a difference between boys and girls?
I know it is physical but in these advanced years why must this be true?
I believe our mental state should be on the beam still I have no clue.
You are tied to your past and children while trying to understand me
And I have the same problem and probably from this we will never be free.
Still I feel we have overcome many past ways and thoughts to be in love
This is because God wanted us to make it together and He is guiding us from
above.
I know many times I hold on to my past stupid ways
And you wonder if we will ever in the future be able to love and play.
I think most of the trouble is our medical history might be tied to our lives
You have your pills and doctors, I have mine so from our pocketbooks money does
make cries.

I don't think that is any real reason not to hold hands and wish for personal help
from above

I really believe God and Washington will help us with cost of prescriptions with
their love.

I believe AARP will prevail in their effort to get Congress to cut prescription drug
cost

If they don't my love holding hands will become the way drug makers will become
our boss.

They will make us pay for there might be germs on our hands

And they will develop a hand wash we must use after holding hands, "Yes they
can!"

I worry about more serious problems of the U.SA. than our hand holding

But I really should not and don't be me scolding.!

You see I don't worry when I am holding your hand at any time

For it drives out all evil thoughts and spirits then I feel fine.

I thank you for being my love and I ramble on

But you are the only one of whom I am so fond.

No. 139

CARING

You have always been there for me
Whether it was a physical pain or an emotional one
I knew you were ready to lend me your strength and loving support.
When you are in the throes of an illness or a worry
And you are downcast, a dark pall over your brilliant spirit,
It hurts me to see your pain and I feel so helpless.
When you withdraw into yourself I miss you;
All I can do is be there when you need me
Hoping you will let me give you love and comfort.
My arms ache to hold you, put your head against my heart,
My hands wanting to soothe your cares away.
You are a deep and private man
Your desire for time alone I respect
And I do not want to intrude.
Just know I am here loving you.

No. 140

IF I AM

I wonder if I am nothing
Why do I get from my love a hugging?
I think I don't really know anything
But she will not let me forget I know everything.
She may be way too much in love
But I rather think this relationship came about from God above.
I squeeze her but she wins in the contest each time
But that is just about super and okay.
Her hazel eyes pierce my mind each time they lock on
I guess I want it that way for of her I am very fond.
I question why she could ever have a thing for me
She is educated and came from a well bred family with a deep family tree.
I came forward as a western country boy
Does that mean the eastern girl with me does a love employ.
I think it quite possible to have any kind of love
As long as God has look down and approved it from above.
I really hate God to approve my love
But if He shouldn't then away it will fly like a white dove.
I could watch TV all night but I know that is not right
Just for moments in our walks her hand I want to hold tight.
I can't explain the flame inside my heart she does light
I know it is love and being with her is perfectly all right.
She can scratch an itch on my back I can't reach
But I think there are a few fun things to her I might teach.
I watch her smile and expressions for a clue
That I can break through.
She tries to get me to be myself in love many times
I just can't do it for I am a fool thinking it might be a crime.

Where will I summon the courage to be myself with her?

I guess I bragged to myself too much and I am the only one heard.

I write to see what I am thinking about this lovely woman in my life

Most of my thoughts are okay and other thoughts could get me in trouble once or twice.

Once there was a famous poet who wrote words of his love for his lover

I guess my best loving words would be better if them I never utter.

The faith and love expressed by my love about me

Makes it at times hard to live up to what she might want me to be,

Finally I realize she is in love with me as much as I am with her

So it becomes important to just be ourselves for that is what we love and on this we concur.

When I write about our love I find myself stumbling for words

I am not a good talker so writing my love is the only way I can be heard.

No. 141

YOU ARE MY HAPPINESS

I look at you and feel so much love;
You make me feel like a teenager again,
Head over heels in love for the first time.
Being with you makes me unbelievably happy,
Sending shivers of excitement through my body.
So unexpectedly a friendship turned to love
You entered my heart as softly as a whisper
Capturing me with your beautiful words of love,
Your eyes and touch telling me of your passion.
Like the last piece of a puzzle you complete me.
Even though they do not know you, my children love you,
Knowing only that with you I am happy and content.
Your children have so graciously made me welcome,
Sharing with me their warmth and a loving family.
I ask only that we spend our remaining years together-
The thought that someday we may be parted threatens to destroy me.
Your loving face and beautiful eyes act as a magnet;
My hands aching to touch you, to hold you close,
My lips needing to kiss you and love you.
When your eyes soften with passion you shatter my self-control.
Having always been so shy, my boldness astonishes me.
You have breached the wall I have always had around.
Loving you so much leaves me vulnerable, but I do not fear-
I know you love me and will not knowingly hurt me.
All the words of those who have been in love
Would not be nearly enough to express my feelings for you.
I adore you—I live for you.

No. 142

SWEET LOVING

Oh, how I love you,
Now more than ever,
My desire for you even stronger.
I can't stop thinking of your sweet loving,
My mind filled with memories of the sensations you created,
Wanting you with a hunger undiminished.
My hands, my lips, my body were made to love you.
I want to make you feel the same sweet sensations,
To make you tremble with wanting me,
To create ripples of excitement to race through your body.
When I love it is with my whole being, without reservation.
I've always tried to be honest with myself;
I realize that though you say you love me,
It may not be with the same emotional investment.
Does my intensity frighten you—I can only hope not.
You fascinate me with your humor,
Your enthusiasm for life and your wonderfully creative mind.
You give life an added enjoyment and make the days sparkle.
As I grow older, there is the feeling of a greater freedom,
A freedom to express my deepest feelings,
To enjoy the surprisingly sensual side of my nature with you.
All this your love has done for me.
Your acceptance of me as I am has made all possible.
Let us make the most of the time that remains to us.

No. 143

IN A FOG

I am each morning in a fog over you
I carry you in my heart each day through.
I start my daily trek on my bike
Wondering how many times you crossed my heart during the night.
Why am I doing this bike ride—it is so dumb?
But I know to continue to live I must so it is for you my Hon!
As my heart doctor put it so bluntly to my face
If you don't exercise you will soon be leaving the human race.
I carry a picture of your love in my heart
So I don't grumble each day I start.
I must admit each day I start in a mental fog
I meet each day different walkers, bikers and those who jog.
I don't think if I didn't have that picture of your love for me
I would even consider all the sweat and some pain but you I deeply want you to please.
I watch many others walk their pets for their health
But I don't have a pet so my bike becomes that item in my collection of wealth.
That I commit to the mental fog each morning is not entirely true
I know with your love each morning why I ride the bike for you.
I suppose when a lover writes to his most favorite person in all the world
It best not be the bike but his loving thoughts of a senior girl.
Being senior lovers isn't really so bad
When together and doing the many things you can makes both of you very glad.
It may be as simple as holding hands while one is waiting to see a doctor about health
Or it may be buying for the other a useless item with love for neither has much wealth.

It can be a look into the other's eyes then feeling that love coming over you like a
fog

It might be while walking along a small pond and being startled by a jumping frog.

It can be all of these things at this point in life as love covers you with blanketing
fog

Yet it might be the realization that both of you now walk together and no longer
jog.

Yes, life is beautiful when you have it to share with someone at any age

Your desires and loves are calm thus within you lose all rage.

My dear, I don't know what else to tell you at this time about my burning love for
you

Just attempting with words to explain it as being true.

No. 144

SECOND GREATEST POEM

The ocean water washed over the beach sand

The moon rose high casting sparkling tips on each wave again and again.

The two lone lovers embraced as they strolled down a moonlit sand beach

They felt the warmth of love spring through their hearts and for each other's heart they did reach.

Where had the special day gone as they had roamed the fields and nearby hills?

Could they ever stand to be separated again with that they had despair in hearts filled?

Their escape to this lonely beach away from all their past stress

For now at last their minds, bodies and hearts could rest.

They had been torn by family, friends and a changing world

For they had turmoil in their lives that had tossed them around in its swirl.

Finally together they had escaped to this unknown place

So it seemed God bound them together with His loving grace.

Now it was for them to continue on what was now their course of life that had been set

They could no longer allow others into their loving life get.

Had they been young lovers then possibly life would have been different in many ways

But No! These senior loves might be counting their remaining days.

No longer would they allow others to interfere with their future destination

They would travel this last road together and never again be alone or impatient.

They were parents of grown children who seemed to approve of this relationship

In fact a couple of the children had approved of this union with great statesmanship.

The two wanted approval of all the children on both sides

But if they didn't get it then "To Hell" it was their life to be lived in their own strides.

Another good point was neither had any great wealth or fortune to leave
So this would never be a problem for the children they did not believe.
Both their former partners had died after several years of ill health
And both had cared for that partner with all their heart and with little help.
When the two of them found each other quite by mistake
It was after the first kiss that their hearts and bodies began to shake.
Each wondered it was possible to love again in the short time they would have on earth
And to their shock and pleasant surprise an emotion in each began to rise.
They had many things in common and enjoyed the same things each day
So God guided them along peacefully in his quiet way.
He seemed to say that each of them had a lot to give to others in the remaining days
So as they blended into a single team it was to be what God wanted we now say.
The man wrote and felt a warm love in his heart so he could again write
And the woman with her overpowering love corrected his writing late into the night.
He felt success finally as it had slipped silently from his grasp over the years
She felt a love for a man who in his writings with her could finally enjoy some cheers.
They embarked on a drive for success in the chance of the publishing game
God smiled on their efforts and provided a limited fame.
Where this relationship and love will go or will in the future is not known
But for once in this love neither of them will ever again be alone.

No. 145

FIRST ENCOUNTER

I wonder as I enter into marriage as a senior guy

What will our first dispute or encounter be over and why?

Will it be something we both did differently in the past

Nor will it be serious or last.

I think not for we have risen to a new height in our lives

I attempted to win with her with shallow tries.

I am a mature man of some cander and mainly learned it doesn't work with my
new mate

So when I goof I will admit my mistake truthfully which I might hate!

I set out to win her hand with a determined effort

I wanted her to know if she would marry me she would be my dessert.

I am not sure about my selection of words in this poem

What I am trying to say is I don't want any longer to be alone.

I want to be with her the rest of my life

For I know as her husband she will be a super wife.

I know I love her so much as I fumble around for the right words

I expect all men in their senior years who fall in love again feel like the so-called
nerd.

We hope and pray for a different love just because of our years

Knowing as we love we attempt many things that nearly bring us to tears.

Parts of our body have worn out or just faded with time

Yet our new senior woman is aware of these failures and they say it is fine.

They love us like a true love should and not like in our younger life

They too have found they have changed much like we have which in a way makes
it nice.

I find myself explaining my stumbling more to myself than to my future mate

And when I have to explain a senior fault to myself is what I hate.

I think I should perform like when I was twenty years of age with my new love

But I guess God determined enough is enough and He did it from above.

We are to move through life on our way to be in His heaven someday

Yet for now He has allowed us to combine in love with His blessing way.

She and I both realize we have had a wonderful life with the mates we lost

Still we must live on and together we have decided it will be without personal cost.

We find we love the same things and we are able to work any problem out

Without a battle that in our first marriage which was many times like a boxing bout.

We now hold hands in the open like a couple of kids

Probably long ago we did and from prying eyes hid.

The only real difference is she has the right to cheat

As I am driving along a road her hand can in my body an excitement create.

I remember the long searches for that lonely parking spot.

Now as a senior lover I can follow her into her home and let her know what I want.

I suppose I could go on and on about the advantages of being a senior man in love

If you are such a senior lover let this poem be the right thing for you and a personal shove.

No. 146

You Don't Forget

You don't forget your life-long mate of the past
Or should you I think that would make your new love not last.
Those loves and thoughts add to your new senior love
For just maybe they are encouraging you now from above.
They want you to be happy while stuck on earth
And a new love or mate is what real life is really worth
Having lost a life-long mate makes one wonder about the future life
But the first thing one has to realize you don't have to make all right.
As a senior lover I find myself wrestling with questions of love in bed at night
I have decided all the years of raising children and having just one love
I was so lucky to have had one lover all the time with the blessing of God above.
Now in my senior years with her gone to be with God
I must now strike out on my own to find another to love.
She appeared before my eyes
Which was when I looked at my co-worker and she was no surprise.
We had both lost a partner of many years
Over them we had with our children shed many tears.
It was now time to move on in our senior life that was for sure
A quick solution was not going to be the cure.
We needed time to heal from our lifetime partner's loss
Still we didn't need to live forever in their shadow's cost.
We needed to be ourselves and we were alive needing to live
Most of all to each other we found we needed to give.
When life ends for one it does not end for another
Especially your mate of many years for they may have been a father or mother.
Your children love you as you pick another senior partner in life
They respond by saying go for it and if the new partner is right then for you it is
nice.

A person questions whether it is right to re-marry in the senior years
It is better than when in silence you cry those many silent lonely tears.
I find only selfish children cry out in pain
That you might try to be happy again.
I think that in time a senior parent should assure them that there is no money left
They had better be happy now or you will send them a bill for the funeral at best.

No. 147

A Night of Love Thoughts

I lie awake on different nights with thoughts floating in my head

What will the poor world do when I am dead?

For you see I put my thoughts on paper for all to read

My thoughts I might be a beggar, a high-flying airplane pilot or a knight on a mighty steed.

I write about truths, many ideas, desires and many dreams

I must write them down and publish them if possible it seems.

Still my fair maiden remains the same one

In time we will be together forever as one, me and my love I call HON!

It becomes funny at times even as two seniors how we blend

I start to say something and she laughs thinking the same so we start again.

We touch hands as we walk most everywhere

As for each other we have a deep loving and care.

It is better in the senior years for you are not bound by foolish thoughts

You don't ask yourself what if and I hadn't ought.

You forge ahead with your love being reckless at times

And don't push or pull your mate wanting all to be so fine.

I have thoughts at night of the wonderful life we have ahead

As I lie there I pinch myself hoping I am not dead.

I get scared like when a youth in love

Could it be not true and her love will fly away on the wings of a dove.

This senior love I have heard very little about its success

I think back to the many I have known who married in senior years and love did the rest.

This senior love is a funny thing you know

Your passion for a love can come but never go.

Having been married many long years with a mate who died

I have wondered if it is okay to love another after the times I cried.

Life has not ended for me or her

We live on loving one another in our senior years holding on to each other's love word.

It is right as senior lovers to enjoy and want each other

Our children understand as they encourage us, me being the father and her a mother.

It is life's battle wanting to live in love again

So that is what we are going to do as a new life for each begins.

Yes, each of us have had those night thoughts of love

Somehow we know God is smiling on us from His place in Heaven above.

No. 148

FALTER

As we marry should either of us falter in health
We will still have each other our greatest wealth.
We will be able to share many great times I am sure
And I get an impression from God that our love is true and pure.
As before marriage we touched and felt a passion for the other
This affection for God and each other after marriage can come out of cover.
I know we both are living on limited time on this earth
But our love is super and so true it will keep us from death's curse.
We want to share this love with others as we help them in their troubles
We both know that is why we were put on this earth to burst for others those
disarray bubbles.
Each time we write or do things for others we gain a new happiness and strength
inside
I finally realized I need you each second, minute, hour and day
And with our marriage I feel a new sense of love and living way.
I wonder each day why God pushed us together
Plus the more we intertwine our lives seem to get much better.
I don't question the love or decision of our Heavenly Father for our future years
For I know now He looked at me a lost soul confused and nearly in tears.
You were searching for a life but not knowing in what direction to strike out
As I awakened to your deep loving I figured you were what life was about.
I wondered if the Florida heat had gotten to me as your hand touched the back of
my neck
Somehow in my manly stupidity I figured I was falling in love with you, BY
HECK!
I want you to know my love for you has been on the rise and uphill since then
I want to hold you each time and kiss your lovely lips again and again.
Well I can tell now I am a senior lover and not a teenager like in the past.

It is funny as you and I compare notes of our teen years we feel like it will always last.

I can't see anything wrong in enjoying the crazy wild feelings of those days.

I bet we would have found each other then but we lived from each other a long ways.

Yes, God has a strange way of bringing the right souls together for one final fling

And now with our pending marriage and life together I know we will sing.

One thing is certain in our future life we will have each other if one of us should falter.

And being together and not alone anymore we will have an emergency caller

I thank God for you and I know you thank Him too

I am about to close this poem for it is getting too long, so I am through!

No. 149

YES, MY LOVE

You have asked me to be your wife
With love and great joy I have said I will!
Never did I think I would marry again
But I cannot imagine my life without you in it.
Blending together our two lives
With our old habits and ways of doing things
May at times be difficult
But I know that with love and humor
Any problems we encounter will be overcome.
We have been close companions for more than 2 years;
I have gotten to know a wonderful, caring and loving man.
No longer in the first flush of youth,
I value your maturity, your wisdom, your compassion.
I look at you and feel your love for me,
My feelings for you passionate and elemental,
The beauty of our love dominating my every thought.
Now in our senior years time grows more precious,
I never thought I would feel the way I do for you,
The wild thoughts about us that run through my mind,
The dreams that wake me, wanting you beside me,
The ache of my need for you winding through me.
Time has not been kind to us, each having some health concerns,
But our hearts are filled with a deep abiding love.
I look forward to spending the remaining years as your wife,
Proud to call you my husband, my love.

No. 150

What Makes Us Tick?

How do you finish a book like this—you don't as life goes on
For each other your senior love grows and of each other you are fond.
You could close with a final poem
But that isn't right for senior love goes on without a true home.
When those left find another mate
Shutting down memories of a passed partner they hate.
They are left and alive they must live on in another love
For that is what God intended from His perch from above.
A senior love can be as wild or splendid as the two want to make it
As each new senior love wants it to be, into each of their ways it must fit.
Closing this book dedicated to senior love is hard to do
For we are still loving and plenty of things are ahead that is true.
So we guess there are no closing words for a senior love book
For excitement and love is ahead for the two of us we hooked.

Carole S and Keith S

0-595-29423-5

www.ingramcontent.com/pod-product-compliance
Lightning Source LLC
Chambersburg PA
CBHW020912290526
45784CB00002BA/519